FINDING PEACE
in
LIFE'S STORMS

More Titles by Charles Spurgeon

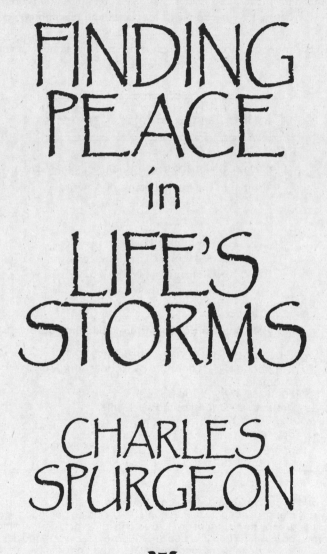

FINDING PEACE in LIFE'S STORMS

CHARLES SPURGEON

WHITAKER
HOUSE

Publisher's note: This new edition from Whitaker House has been updated for the modern reader. Words, expressions, and sentence structure have been revised for clarity and readability.

All Scripture quotations are taken from the King James Version (KJV) of the Holy Bible.

Finding Peace in Life's Storms

ISBN-13: 978-0-88368-479-5 • ISBN-10: 0-88368-479-9
Printed in the United States of America
© 1997 by Whitaker House

Whitaker House
1030 Hunt Valley Circle
New Kensington, PA 15068
www.whitakerhouse.com

Library of Congress Cataloging-in-Publication Data

Spurgeon, C. H. (Charles Haddon), 1834–1892
    Finding peace in life's storms / by Charles Spurgeon.
    p. cm.
    ISBN 0-88368-479-9 (trade paper)
    1. Christian life—Baptist authors.   I. Title.
BV4501.2.S71417 1997
248.4'861—dc21
                                      97-34164
                                        CIP

8 9 10 11 12 13 14 15 **ພ** 16 15 14 13 12 11 10 09

Contents

1

Saved in Hope

We are saved by hope: but hope that is seen is not hope: for what a man seeth, why doth he yet hope for? But if we hope for that we see not, then do we with patience wait for it.
—Romans 8:24–25

We who are believers are saved right now. In a certain sense, we are completely saved. We are entirely saved from the guilt of sin. The Lord Jesus took our sin and bore it in His own body on the cross. He offered an acceptable atonement that did away with the iniquity of all His people once and for all. The penalty of sin has been paid for by our great Substitute and, by faith, we have accepted His sacrifice. *"He that believeth on him is not condemned"* (John 3:18).

When we receive Christ by faith, we are immediately saved from the defilement of evil and have free access to God our Father. By faith, we are saved from the ruling power of sin in our lives. As Romans 6:14 says, *"Sin shall not have dominion over you: for ye are not under the law, but under grace."* In the heart of every Christian, the crown has been removed from the head of sin and the strength of its arm has been broken by the power of faith. Sin strives to gain control, but it cannot win the victory, for he who is born of God does not delight in committing sin. He does not sin as a daily habit. Instead, the believer guards and protects himself so that the Evil One does not touch him.

Now, the Scripture passage that we will be focusing on comes from the eighth chapter of Romans, and it reads, *"We are saved by hope."* However, this does not seem to agree with other parts of Holy Scripture. Everywhere in the Word of God we are told that we are saved by faith. For example, Romans 5:1 says, *"Therefore being justified by faith."* Faith, not hope, is the saving grace, except that in some respects hope is equivalent to faith. In the original Greek, the meaning of Romans 8:24 is, "We were saved *in* hope." If the passage were translated in this way, it would prevent misunderstanding. As the distinguished commentator, Bengel, said,

> The words do not describe the means, but the manner of salvation. We are so saved that there may even yet remain something for which we may hope, both of salvation and glory.

Believers receive the salvation of their souls as the culmination of their faith. They receive salvation by faith, so that they may also receive it by grace. We are saved *by* faith and *in* hope.

Therefore, we rejoice right now in the salvation that we have already obtained and that we already enjoy by faith in Christ Jesus. Yet, we are conscious that there is something more than this to be obtained.

We will receive salvation in a larger sense that we do not yet see. For, at the present moment, we find ourselves living inside temporary tabernacles. *"For we that are in this tabernacle do groan, being burdened"* (2 Cor. 5:4). And, all around us, creation is clearly experiencing labor pains. We can see signs of the earth's contractions in the unrest, upheaval, and anguish occurring in nature.

Things are not the way God originally made them. Thorns are growing in earth's plowed fields; a disease has fallen on her flowers; there is mildew on her grain. The heavens weep and saturate our harvests; the depths of the earth move and shake our cities with earthquakes. Frequent tragedies and disasters foreshadow a great future that will be born as a result of these labor pains.

Nowhere on earth can a perfect paradise be found. Even the best things of our world point to something better. And all of creation groans with us in the pains of labor. Even we who have received the firstfruits of the Spirit and are blessed and saved, groan within ourselves, waiting for something further, a glory not yet seen. We have not yet attained salvation but are pressing on. The first thirstiness of our parched, sinful souls has been quenched, but we have still greater desires within us. We hunger and thirst for righteousness with insatiable longings. Before we ate of the Bread of Heaven, we were hungry for the equivalent of pig slop. Now, however, our newborn nature has brought us a new appetite, which the whole world could not satisfy.

What is the cause of this hunger? That is not a difficult question to answer. Our griefs, longings, and unsatisfied desires fall under two general areas.

First, we long to be totally free from sin in every form. Second, we long to be free from our physical bodies and to receive our resurrected bodies.

Longing for Freedom from Sin

We are burdened by the evil that is in the world. We are troubled by the evil conversations of the ungodly, and we are grieved by their temptations and persecutions. The fact that *"the whole world lieth in wickedness"* (1 John 5:19) and that people reject Christ and perish in unbelief is a source of great distress to us. We could even wish to live in a deserted area, far from civilization, so that we might commune with God in peace and never hear anything more about blasphemy, murmuring, depravity, and crime. This world is not our home, for it is polluted. We are looking for a great deliverance when we will be taken out of this world to dwell in perfect fellowship with others.

Yet, even the presence of the ungodly would be a small matter if we could be completely delivered from sin within ourselves. This is among the *"things not seen"* (Heb. 11:1) that will be fulfilled at a later time. If a person were free from all tendency to sin, he would not be liable to temptation any longer. He would not need to guard against it. If something cannot possibly be burned or blackened, fire cannot hurt it. However, we feel that we must avoid temptation because we are conscious that there are logs or kindling within us that may soon catch fire. Our Lord said, *"The prince of this world cometh, and hath nothing in me"* (John 14:30). But when the Enemy comes to us, he finds not only something, but much that is compatible with his purposes. Our hearts all too readily echo the voice of Satan. When he sows his weeds, the fields of our old natures soon produce a harvest. Evil remains even in those who have been redeemed, and it infects all the faculties of their minds.

Oh, if only we could get rid of the memory of sin! What a torment it is for us to remember dirty words and snatches of obscene songs. If only we were free of sin in our thought lives! Do we mourn enough over sins in our thoughts and imaginations? A person may sin, and sin horribly, in his thoughts, even though he may not sin in his actions. Many people have committed fornication, adultery, theft, and even murder in their imaginations by finding pleasure in the thought of them, and yet they may never have fallen into any of these sins in an overt way. If only our imaginations and our whole inner natures were purged of the corruption that is in them and which ferments into something rancid.

There is evil inside us that makes us exclaim from day to day, *"O wretched man that I am! who shall deliver me from the body of this death?"* (Rom. 7:24). If anyone reading this book is saying, "I never feel that way," I pray to God that he may soon experience it. Those who are content with themselves know very little about true spiritual perfection. A healthy child grows, and so does a healthy child of God. The nearer we come to perfect cleanness of heart, the more we will mourn over the tiniest spot of sin and the more we will recognize as sin things that we once excused. He who is most like Christ is most conscious of imperfection and is impatient to be rid of the least sin. When someone says, "I have reached the goal," I am very concerned for him, for I believe he has not yet begun to run.

11

As for me, I endure many growing pains and feel far less pleased with myself than I used to. I have a firm hope of something better, but if it were not for hope, I would consider myself truly unhappy to be so conscious of my need and so racked with desires. Therefore, this is one major source of our spiritual groaning. We are saved, but we are not completely delivered from tendencies to sin. Neither have we reached the fullness of holiness. *"There remaineth yet very much land to be possessed"* (Josh. 13:1).

Longing for Our Resurrected Bodies

Another reason for this "winter of our discontent" is our bodies. Paul called the body *"vile"* (Phil. 3:21), and indeed it is, when compared to what it will be when it is formed in the image of Christ Jesus. It is not vile in itself, viewed as the creation of God, for it is fearfully and wonderfully made (Ps. 139:14). There is something very noble about the body of man, who has been created to walk on two feet and to look upward and to gaze toward heaven. A body that has been so marvelously prepared to house the mind and to obey the soul's commands is not to be despised. A body that can be the temple of the Holy Spirit is no lowly structure; therefore, let us not despise it. We should be eternally grateful that we have been made human beings—that is, if we also have been made new in Christ Jesus and have *"put on the new man"* (Eph. 4:24). The body came under the power of death through the Fall, and it remains under its power. Because of this, it is destined to die sooner or later, unless the Lord suddenly returns. And, even then, the body must be changed, for flesh and blood, in its present state, cannot inherit the kingdom of God.

And so, our poor bodies are not well matched with our newborn souls, since they have not yet been born again. They are somewhat dull and dreary dwellings for heaven-born spirits! With their aches and pains; weariness and infirmity; need of sleep, food, and clothing; susceptibility to cold, heat, accident, and decay, as well as to excessive labor and exhausting toil, they are pitifully incapable of serving those who are sanctified. They drag down and hinder spirits that otherwise might soar to great heights. Consider how often bad health snuffs out the noble flame of high resolve and holy desires. Think about how often pain and weakness freeze the cheerful streams of the soul. When will we be freed from the chains of this natural body and put on the wedding dress of the spiritual body? Since sin dwells in our hearts and we are clothed in mortal clay, we are glad that our salvation is nearer to us now than when we first believed, and we long to enter into the full enjoyment of it.

Our Scripture text gives us a great amount of encouragement about this. There will come a time when we will be fully delivered from the cause of our present groaning. We will receive a salvation so wide that it will cover all of our needs and even all our desires. A salvation awaits us whose parameters are immense and eternal. Anything we could wish for is encompassed within it. This is what our text is talking about when it says, *"We are saved by hope."* By hope, we have taken hold of this great and wide salvation.

In light of all this, I want to describe for you the kind of hope that has a firm grip on the greater salvation that we are longing for.

Finding Peace in Life's Storms

The Goal of Our Hope

Complete Perfection

Our hope, first of all, is in our own complete perfection in Christ. We have set our faces toward holiness, and by God's grace we will never rest until we attain it. Every sin that is in us is doomed, not only to be conquered, but to be put to death. The grace of God does not help us to hide our sins but to destroy them.

We are to deal with sin as Joshua dealt with the five enemy kings when they hid in the cave at Makkedah. While Joshua was busy with the battle, he said, *"Roll great stones upon the mouth of the cave"* (Josh. 10:18). For a while, our sins are shut up by restraining grace, as in a cave. Great stones are rolled at the cave's mouth, for our sins would escape if they could and once more snatch at the reins of our lives. However, we intend to deal with them more effectively later on in the power of the Holy Spirit. When Joshua said, *"Bring out those five kings unto me"* (Josh. 10:22), he struck and killed them and then hanged them. By God's grace, we will never be satisfied until we hate and denounce all our natural inclinations to sin and they are utterly destroyed. We hope in expectation for a day when not a taint of past sin or an inclination for future sin will remain in us. We will still retain free will and freedom of choice, but we will choose only good. Believers who are now in heaven are not passive beings who are driven along the path of obedience by a power that they cannot resist. As intelligent beings with free wills, they freely choose to be holy before

14

the Lord. We too will enjoy forever the glorious liberty of the children of God, which is found in constantly choosing what is good and right. In this way, we will experience unbroken happiness. Ignorance will no longer exist, for we will all be taught by the Lord and will know as we are known. We will be perfect in our service to God and completely delivered from all self-will and the desires of the flesh; we will be near to our God and will be like Him. As Isaac Watts has written:

> Sin, my worst enemy before,
> Shall vex my eyes and ears no more;
> My inward foes shall all be slain,
> Nor Satan break my peace again.

What a heaven this will be! I think that if I could become absolutely free from every tendency to sin, I would not care where I lived—on earth or in heaven, at the bottom of the sea with Jonah or in the low dungeon with Jeremiah. Purity is peace; holiness is happiness. He who is holy as God is holy will be happy as God is happy. This is the chief goal of our hope.

The Redemption of Our Bodies

Another goal is the redemption of our bodies. Read the verses in which Paul taught that truth:

> *And if Christ be in you, the body is dead because of sin; but the Spirit is life because of righteousness. But if the Spirit of him that raised up Jesus from the dead dwell in you, he that raised up Christ from the dead shall also quicken your mortal bodies by his Spirit that dwelleth in you.* (Rom. 8:10–11)

When we die, we will leave our bodies behind for a while. We will not, therefore, in regard to our entire beings, be perfect until the resurrection. We will be morally perfect, but since a complete person is made up of body and soul, we will not be physically perfect while one part of us remains in the tomb. When the resurrection trumpet sounds, our bodies will rise, but they will rise in a redeemed state. Our regenerated spirits are very different from what our spirits were when they were under the bondage of sin. In the same way, when our bodies are resurrected, they will be greatly different from what they are now.

The diseases caused by sickness and age will be unknown among glorified believers, for they will be as the angels of God. No one will enter into glory lame, maimed, frail, or deformed. No one will be blind or deaf. There will be no paralysis or wasting away from tuberculosis. We will possess everlasting youth. The body that is sown in weakness will be raised in power and will immediately obey the commands of its Lord. Paul said, *"It is sown a natural [soulish] body"* (1 Cor. 15:44), appropriate for the soul, and *"it is raised a spiritual body"* (v. 44), appropriate for the spirit, the highest nature of man. I suppose we will inhabit the kind of body that cherubim wear when they fly *"upon the wings of the wind"* (2 Sam. 22:11), or the kind of body that seraphim inhabit when, like *"a flame of fire"* (Heb. 1:7), they rush to obey Jehovah's commands. Whatever they will be, our poor bodies will be very different from what they are now. At present, they are shriveled bulbs that will be put into the earth. But they will rise as glorious flowers, golden cups to hold the sunlight of Jehovah's face.

We do not yet know the greatness of their glory, except that they will be formed like the glorious body of the Lord Jesus. Therefore, this is the second goal of our hope, that we will receive glorified bodies that will be able to unite with our purified spirits.

Our Spiritual Inheritance

Viewed in another light, the goal of our hope is that we will enter into our spiritual inheritance. Paul said, *"If children, then heirs; heirs of God, and joint-heirs with Christ"* (Rom. 8:17). Whether we own only a little or a great amount in this life, our estates are nothing compared to what God holds in trust for us, what He has pledged that we will receive on the Day when we will come of age. The fullness of God is the heritage of believers. All that can make a person blessed and noble and complete is reserved for us. Measure, if you can, the inheritance of Christ, who is Heir of all things! What must be the portion of the well-beloved Son of the Highest? Whatever it is, it is ours, for we are joint-heirs with Christ. We will be with Him and see His glory; we will wear His image; we will sit on His throne. I cannot tell you more, for my words are poverty-stricken. I wish that we would all meditate on what the Scripture reveals about this subject until we know everything that can be known about it. Our hope looks for many things; it looks for everything. Rivers of pleasure, of pleasures forevermore, are flowing for us at God's right hand.

Paul wrote of *"the glory which shall be revealed in us"* (Rom. 8:18). He said that it is *"a far more exceeding and eternal weight of glory"* (2 Cor. 4:17).

17

Glory—what a word! Glory is to be our ours, even though we are poor sinners. Grace is sweet but what must glory be? And this glory is to be revealed in us, around us, over us, and through us, for all eternity.

Paul also wrote of *"the glorious liberty of the children of God"* (Rom. 8:21). *Liberty* is such a delightful word! We love the idea of liberty, especially when we hear the sounds of freedom coming from the silver bugles of those who fight with tyrants. But what will it be like when the trumpets of heaven proclaim eternal freedom to every spiritual slave! There is no comparison between human and heavenly liberty, the liberty of the children of God. We will have the freedom to enter into the Holy of Holies, to dwell in God's presence, and to see His face forever and ever.

The apostle also spoke of *"the manifestation of the sons of God"* (v. 19). Here on earth, we are hidden away in Christ as gems in a jewelry box. Later on, we are to be revealed as jewels in a crown. Christ was revealed to the Gentiles after He had been hidden for a while. In the same way, we who are presently unknown are to be revealed before men and angels. *"Then shall the righteous shine forth as the sun in the kingdom of their Father"* (Matt. 13:43). I cannot tell you what this manifestation will be like. *"Eye hath not seen, nor ear heard, neither have entered into the heart of man, the things which God hath prepared for them that love him"* (1 Cor. 2:9). And, although *"God hath revealed them unto us by his Spirit"* (v. 10), our spirits have been able to receive only a small part of this revelation.

I suppose that only someone who has had the privilege of seeing the eternal home of those who have been perfected in Christ can tell us what it is like. And I imagine that even he could not do so, for language could not describe it. When Paul was in paradise, he heard words, but he did not tell us what they were, for he said that it was not lawful for a man to speak them. They were too divine for mortal tongues to speak.

Not yet, but later on, the object of our hope will be revealed to us. Do not think less of it because it will come in the future, for the interval of time is inconsequential. What are a few months or years? What if a few hundred years intervene before we are resurrected? They will quickly sweep by us, like the wing of a bird, and then! Oh, then! The invisible will be seen; the unutterable will be heard; eternal life will be ours forever and ever. This is our hope.

The Nature of Our Hope

Now, this hope in which we are saved consists of three things: belief, desire, and expectancy.

Our hope of being completely delivered from sin in our spirits and of being rescued from all sickness in our bodies, arises out of a solemn assurance of our salvation. The revelation of Him who has brought life and immortality to light, bears witness to us that we also will obtain glory and immortality. We will be raised in the image of Christ and will share in His glory. This is our belief because we know that Christ has been raised and glorified and that we are one with Him.

We not only believe this, but we fervently desire it. We desire it so much that, at times, we want to die so that we may enter into it. All the time, but especially when we get a glimpse of Christ, our souls long to be with Him.

This desire is accompanied by confident expectation. We expect to see the glory of Christ and to share in it, as much as we expect to see tomorrow morning. Actually, we may not live to see the sun tomorrow morning, but we will certainly see the King in His beauty in the land that is very far away.

We believe it, we desire it, and we expect it. That is the nature of our hope. It is not an indefinite, hazy, groundless wish that things will turn out all right, such as when people say, "I hope things will go well for me," even though they live carelessly and do not seek God. Rather, it is a hope that is made up of accurate knowledge, firm belief, spiritual desire, and an expectancy that is fully warranted.

This hope is grounded on the Word of God. God has promised us complete salvation; therefore, we believe in it, desire it, and expect it. Jesus has said, *"He that believeth and is baptized shall be saved"* (Mark 16:16). The widest meaning that we can give to the word *saved* must be God's meaning for it, since His thoughts are always above our thoughts. We expect God to do what He has said, to the fullest extent of His promise, for He will never back off from His word or fail to keep His commitments. We have committed our souls to the care of the Savior, who has declared that He will save His people from their sins. We are trusting in our Redeemer.

For I know that my redeemer liveth, and that he shall stand at the latter day upon the earth: and though after my skin worms destroy this body, yet in my flesh shall I see God.
(Job 19:25–26)

Our bodies will be raised imperishable. The Word of God contains many more precious words to the same effect, and we hold onto them, certain that what God has promised He also is able to carry out. We will die without any doubt that we will rise again, even as we have already committed to the dust many of our loved ones in the firm and certain hope of their resurrection to eternal life. The farmer drops his seed into the ground and does not doubt that he will see it rise again. Similarly, we bury the bodies of believers and will eventually resign our own bodies to the grave in the certain expectation that they will live again as surely as they have lived at all. This is a hope worth having, for it is grounded on the Word of God, the faithfulness of God, and His power to carry out His own promise. Therefore, we have a very sure and steadfast hope, and no one who has it will be put to shame.

This hope is stirred up within us by the Spirit of God. We would never have known this hope if the Holy Spirit had not awakened it in our hearts. Ungodly people have no such hope and never will have. It is only when people are renewed that this hope enters into them, since then the Holy Spirit dwells in them. And, because of this, I rejoice with unspeakable joy. If my hope of perfection and immortality has been instilled in me by God, then it has to be fulfilled, for the Lord never would inspire a hope that would put His people to shame. The true God never gave mankind a false hope. That could never happen. The God of hope, who has taught you to expect salvation from sin and all its effects, will do for you according to the expectation that He Himself has inspired. Therefore, be very confident and patiently wait for the joyful Day when the Lord will appear.

This hope operates within us in a holy manner, as every gracious and holy thing that comes from God must do. It purifies us, as John said: *"And every man that hath this hope in him purifieth himself, even as he is pure"* (1 John 3:3). We are so certain of this inheritance that we prepare for it by putting off all things that are contrary to it and putting on all things that suit it. We try to live in the prospect of glory.

How often it has occurred to me (and, I imagine, to you) to say, regarding something, "How will this look in the Day of Judgment?" We have acted generously or consecrated ourselves, not because we cared anything about what people would think of it but because we looked at it in the light of the coming glory. Our greatest motivation is that a crown of life is reserved for us that will never fade.

This blessed hope makes us feel that it is shameful for us to sin, shameful that princes and princesses of the royal bloodline should play in the mire like children of the gutter. Instead, we willingly live as those who are destined to live forever in inexpressible light. We cannot walk in darkness, for we are to live in a splendor that makes the sun seem pale. We are to be immersed in the fellowship of the Trinity. Should we, therefore, be the slaves of Satan or the servants of sin? God forbid! This blessed hope draws us toward God and lifts us out of the pit of sin.

Anticipating Our Hope

In reality, we have already received the greater salvation about which I have been writing. This occurred when we first understood and accepted the hope of eternal life. By faith, we have obtained the first part of salvation, which is forgiveness from sin and justification through Christ. And, by faith, we also have fellowship with God and access into His countless blessings. Some of us are as conscious of this as we are of eating and drinking. But, besides all this, through our hope, we have received the down payment of the fuller range of salvation, which is total deliverance from sin and the complete redemption of our bodies from pain and death. We have this salvation in hope and we *"rejoice in hope of the glory of God"* (Rom. 5:2). Now, what does all this mean?

In our hope, we saw that salvation had been secured for us by the promise of grace. As soon as we believed in Christ, our faith secured forgiveness for us, and we exclaimed, "We are not yet free from our tendency to sin, but since we have believed in Christ for salvation, we will surely be perfected. He could not have come to give us a partial and imperfect salvation. He will perfect everything that concerns us." In hope, we saw within the promise of salvation much that we have not yet experienced. Knowing that the entire promise is equally certain, we expect the future mercy as surely as, in faith, we are enjoying the present blessing.

Moreover, in hope, we saw the promise of the full harvest in the firstfruits. Sin has been subdued by grace, but we expect to see it utterly exterminated. When the Holy Spirit came to dwell within us, our hope concluded that the body would be delivered as surely as the soul had been. The moment that faith introduced hope into the heart, hope said, "I have complete salvation—not in the sense that I am experiencing it now, but Christ Jesus holds it in trust for me."

Finding Peace in Life's Storms

As the priest in the Old Testament waved the sheaf of the firstfruits before the Lord as an acceptable sacrifice, we, in hope, offered the firstfruits of our faith to God and so took possession of the full harvest of salvation. When God gave you and me a love for Jesus and deliverance from the dominion of evil, these firstfruits signified a perfect salvation that has yet to be revealed in us. Our first joy in salvation was like a tuning of our harps for everlasting song. Our first peace was like the dawning light of a never ending day. When we first saw Christ and worshipped Him, our adoration was our initial bowing before the throne of God and of the Lamb. Therefore, in hope we were saved. Hope brought us the source of perfection, the pledge of immortality, the beginnings of glorification.

Moreover, in hope, we are so sure about this coming blessing that we consider it already obtained. Suppose you get a confirmation from a trader with whom you have conducted overseas business. He says, "I have procured the goods you have ordered and will send them by the next ship, which will probably arrive at such and such a time." Then another trader calls and asks you if you want to buy the same kind of goods, and you reply, "No, I already have them." Have you spoken the truth? Certainly, for although you do not have them in your warehouse, they have been invoiced to you. You know that they are on the way, and you are so used to trusting your foreign trader that you regard the goods as yours. The agreement has been made that makes them yours.

It is the same way with heaven, perfection, and immortality. The deed has been done that makes these the heritage of believers. We have confirmation from One whom we cannot doubt, our Lord Jesus, that He has gone to heaven to prepare a place for us and that He will come again and receive us to Himself. In hope, we are so sure of this fact that we consider it done. We may also draw practical conclusions from our hope.

A good old proverb tells us, "Never count your chickens before they are hatched." However, in this case, you may count the chickens just as accurately while the birds are in their eggs, as when they are hatched, for the apostle said, *"I reckon that the sufferings of this present time are not worthy to be compared with the glory which shall be revealed in us"* (Rom. 8:18). He was so sure of the hope of eternal life that he kept an account. He put down the sufferings of his life in his expenditure column and placed the glory that will be revealed among his assets. He declared that his assets were vast, but that his expenditures were so utterly insignificant that they were not worth noticing.

Moreover, the apostle Paul was so sure that he would receive his inheritance that he yearned for it intensely. We who are in this body groan for our full adoption as children of God. Our groanings do not arise from doubt but from eagerness. Our confident anticipation causes us to have an intense desire to receive what we have been promised. It is useless to cry for what you will never have. The child who cries because he cannot have the moon is foolish. But to groan for what I am certain to receive is proper and appropriate and shows the strength of my faith.

The apostle was so sure of receiving the hope of his salvation that he triumphed in it. He said that we are *"more than conquerors through him that loved us"* (Rom. 8:37). In other words, although we are not yet perfect, and although our bodies have not yet been delivered from pain, we are so sure of perfection and complete deliverance that we joyfully endure all things, triumphing over every difficulty.

Friend, you will not be poor much longer. You will live where the streets are paved with gold. Your head will not ache much longer, for it will wear a crown of glory and bliss. Do not allow shame or embarrassment to bother you, for people will not be able to laugh at you much longer. You will be at the right hand of God the Father, and the glory of Christ will clothe you forever. It is an infinite blessing that we have such a hope, and are so sure of it that we anticipate its joys before they actually come to us. Yes, we were saved in hope.

The Sphere of Our Hope

The sphere of hope is *"things not seen"* (Heb. 11:1). As our Scripture text says, *"Hope that is seen is not hope: for what a man seeth, why doth he yet hope for?"* Therefore, a Christian's real possession is not what he sees. Suppose that God prospers him in this world and he has riches. Let him be grateful, but let him confess that these are not his treasure. One hour with the Lord Jesus Christ will bring more satisfaction to the believer than the largest amount of wealth. Although the believer may prosper in this world, he will ridicule the idea of making the world his inheritance. A thousand worlds, with all the joy that they could yield, are nothing compared to our promised inheritance. Our hope does not concern

itself with insignificant things. It leaves the mice of
the barn to the owls and soars on eagle's wings
where nobler joys are waiting to be received.

> Beyond, beyond this lower sky,
>   Up where eternal ages roll;
> Where solid pleasures never die,
>   And fruits immortal feast the soul.

However, it is clear that at the present time we
do not enjoy these glorious things for which we hope.
The unbeliever exclaims, "Where is your hope?" and
we confess that we do not see the objects of our hope.
For instance, we cannot claim to be perfect already.
Neither do we expect to be perfect while we are in
this body. But we believe that we will be perfected in
the image of Christ at the time appointed by the Father. By no means are our bodies free from sickness
right now. Aches and pains and weariness remind us
that our bodies are under the power of death because of sin. Yet, our firm conviction is that we will
wear the heavenly image, just as we now wear the
earthly image.

These are subjects of hope and, therefore, they
are beyond our present experience. Let us not be discouraged about this. Hope must have something to
feed on. We cannot have all of heaven and yet remain on earth. My dear believer, if you feel tormented by sin within you and your holiness seems
battered and spotted, you can be fully persuaded
that He who has promised complete salvation is able
to do it.

Do not judge yourself any longer by what you
do, what you see, what you feel, or what you are.

Rise into the sphere of the things that will be. When there is no joy in the present, you can know that there is infinite joy in the future. Do not say, "Oh, but that is a long way off." That is not true. Many who are reading this book may be sixty, seventy, or even eighty years old. Your time to be with Christ cannot be far away, for the thread of your lives is snapping. Some of us are middle-aged, but since we have already reached the average age of life, we have to acknowledge that our lease will soon run out also. And, since so many people are snatched away in their prime, we may at any moment be caught up to the land for which we hope.

We should not worry about what we will do ten years from now, for it is very likely that by that time we will have entered into the promised rest. We will be serving the Lord day and night in His temple and will be gazing on His face with unspeakable joy. Even if some of us should be doomed to exile from heaven for another fifty years, the time will soon fly away.

Let us work to our utmost for the glory of God while we are still here on earth, for the moments slip away. Do you remember this time last year? It seems like it was only the other day. Boys and girls think that a year is a long time, but older folks have a different opinion. The years no longer seem long to us, now that we are growing gray. For me, time travels so fast that its axles are hot with speed.

Fear exclaims, "Oh, for a little breathing room!" But Hope answers, "No, let the years fly away, for then we will be home all the sooner."

There is only a step between us and heaven. Let us not worry about things below. We are like people on an express train who see a disagreeable sight out the window; it is gone before they have time to think about it. And, if they experience some discomfort along the way, if they have been put into a third-class compartment when they had a first-class ticket, they do not worry about it if it is a short journey. "Never mind," they say. "We have just passed the last station and will be in the terminal shortly."

Let us project ourselves into the future. We do not need much dynamite of imagination to send us there. We can leap that little distance by hope and seat ourselves among the thrones above. Resolve, at least for today, that you will not linger in a cloudy, earthbound frame of mind, but will mount to the bright, cloudless eternity. Oh, to leave these muddy streams and bathe in the river of hope whose crystal waters flow from the pure fountain of divine joy.

The Effect of Our Hope

Now let us look at the effect of our hope, which our Scripture text describes in this way: *"We with patience wait for it."* We wait, and we must wait, but not like criminals awaiting their execution. We wait like a bride anticipating her wedding. We wait with patience, constancy, desire, and submission. The joy is sure to come; we have no doubt about it. Therefore, we do not complain and grumble, as if God had missed His appointment and had delayed us unnecessarily. No, the time that God has decided is the best, and we are content with it.

We neither desire to linger here nor to depart at any time but the Lord's appointed time. Rowland Hill, the English postal reformer, is said to have searched out an aged friend who was dying, so that he could send a message to his friends in heaven. He playfully added a word of hope that the Master had not forgotten old Rowland and would let him come home in due time. Yet, he never dreamed that he could actually be left behind. Among the last expressions of the famous John Donne was this: "I were miserable if I might not die." This would be a horrible world, indeed, if we were doomed to live in it forever. Imagine such a terrible reality.

I met a man some time ago who told me that he would never die, but would, at certain intervals, throw off the effects of age and start on a new phase of life. He kindly came to tell me how I could enjoy the same thing, but since I have no ambition for earthly immortality, such an offer did not tempt me. He told me I could renew my youth and become young again for hundreds of years, but I declined the gift at any price. I have no desire for anything of the sort. My most comfortable prospect about this life is that it will melt away into eternal life.

It seems to me that the most joyful thing about the most joyful life here on earth is that it leads upward to a different and better state. I am not unhappy or discontented, but since I have a good hope that my soul and body will be perfected, and a sure prospect of face-to-face fellowship with God, how can I speak well of anything that divides me from my joy?

Yes, eternal life will surely come; therefore, let us patiently wait for it. When Satan attacks us, when temptation threatens to overcome us, when affliction wears us down, when doubts torment us, let us stand firm and bear the temporary trial, for we will soon be out of range of gunshot. The consummation will come; it has to come, and when it comes we will no longer remember our suffering. We will be filled with joy that our heaven has been born to us and we to it.

Now, then, if you do not believe in God, tell me what your hope is. Make it known in the world and let everyone evaluate it. What is your hope? To live long? Yes, and then what? To bring up a family? Yes, and then what? To see your children comfortably settled in life? Yes, and then what? To be the grandparent of numerous grandchildren? Yes, and then what? To reach extreme old age in peaceful retirement? Yes, and then what? The curtain falls. Let me lift it. The cemetery. The throne of God. Your spirit is sentenced. The trumpet of the resurrection sounds. Final doom. Body and spirit in hell forever.

Without Christ, you have no better prospect than that. I implore you to open your eyes and see what is to be seen. May the Lord have mercy on you and give you a better hope. As for you who believe in Christ, I urge you to begin today to sing the songs of eternal life. Ease your pilgrim life with songs of hope.

2

The Anchor of Your Soul

*Wherein God, willing more abundantly to show unto
the heirs of promise the immutability of his counsel,
confirmed it by an oath: that by two immutable
things, in which it was impossible for God to lie, we
might have a strong consolation, who have fled for
refuge to lay hold upon the hope set before us: which
hope we have as an anchor of the soul, both sure and
stedfast, and which entereth into that within the veil;
whither the forerunner is for us entered, even Jesus,
made an high priest for ever after the
order of Melchisedec.*
Hebrews 6:17–20

Faith is the divinely appointed way of receiving the blessings of grace. One of the main declarations of the Gospel is, *"He that believeth...shall be saved"* (Mark 16:16). The wonders of creation, the disclosures of divine revelation, and the workings of providence are all intended to create and encourage the principle of faith in the living God. When God reveals anything, He wants us to believe it. It is true of all the books of Holy Scripture that *"these are written, that ye might believe...and that believing ye might have life"* (John 20:31).

33

If God conceals anything, He does so to cause us to trust in Him. What we already know leaves little room for trust. Conversely, we have to depend on Him for what we do not know. Providence sends us various trials and all of them are for the purpose of exercising and increasing our faith. At the same time, in answer to prayer, providence brings us a variety of proofs of the faithfulness of God, and these evidences serve to refresh our faith.

In this way, the works and the words of God cooperate to educate men in the grace of faith. You might presume, however, from the doctrine of certain teachers, that the Gospel message is, "Whosoever *doubts* will be saved," and that nothing could be more useful or honorable than for a person's mind to hang in perpetual suspense, for him to be sure of nothing, confident of the truth of no one, not even of God Himself.

The Bible gives a eulogy to the memory of its heroes, and it writes as their epitaph, *"These all died in faith"* (Heb. 11:13). However, the modern gospel ridicules faith and establishes the new virtue of keeping up with the very latest thought of the age. Simple trust in the truthfulness of God's Word, which our ancestors taught was the basis of all faith, seems to be at a discount now with so-called learned men and women who are able to handle "modern thinking."

It is shameful that some ministers who profess Christ are worshipping at this shrine and are working hard to gain the reputation of being intellectual and philosophical by scattering doubts everywhere. The doctrine of the "blessedness of doubt" is as opposed to the Gospel of Jesus Christ as darkness is to light or as Satan is to Christ Himself. It has been invented to quiet the consciences of proud men and women who refuse to yield their minds to God's rule.

Have faith in God, for faith is, in itself, a virtue of the highest order. No virtue is more truly excellent than simple confidence in the Eternal, which a person is enabled to exhibit by the grace of the Holy Spirit. And not only is faith a virtue in itself, it is the origin of all virtues. A person who believes God gains strength for work, patience for suffering, wholeheartedness for love, earnestness for obedience, and zealousness for service. Faith is the root from which all that can beautify the human character grows. Far from being opposed to good works, faith is the ever flowing fountain from which they proceed. Take faith away from a person who professes Christ, and you have cut off the source of his strength; as with Samson, you have cut his hair and left him with no power either to defend himself or to conquer his enemies.

"The just shall live by faith" (Rom. 1:17). Faith is essential to the vitality of Christianity, and anything that weakens faith weakens the chief source of spiritual power. My friend, not only does our own experience teach us this, and the Word of God declare it, but all of human history is an example of the same truth. Faith is force. Why, even when people have been mistaken, if they have believed the mistake, they have displayed more power than people who have known the truth but have not wholeheartedly believed it. The influence that a person has in dealing with his fellowmen lies very much in the force of conviction that his beliefs have over his own soul.

If you teach a person the truth so that he believes it with his whole heart, then you have given him both the capability and the tools with which he may move the world. To this day, the whole earth trembles under the footsteps of Martin Luther. Why? He was strong in faith. Luther was a living believer. The academics with whom he had to contend were mere disputers, and the priests and cardinals and popes with whom he came into contact were mere dealers in dead traditions; therefore, he struck down their ideas unsparingly and with great devastation. With his whole being he believed in what he had learned from God. Revelation 2:27 says, *"He shall rule them with a rod of iron; as the vessels of a potter shall they be broken."* That was the way Martin Luther was. As an iron rod among potters' vessels, he smashed to pieces the pretenders of his age.

What has been true in history all along is most certainly true now. It is by believing that we become strong. That is clear enough. Whatever supposed excellence there may be in the much-prized qualities of being open-minded, having a cultured intellect, or maintaining the unsettled judgment of honest disbelief, I am unable to discern them. I see no reference to these things in Scripture.

The Bible does not praise unbelief nor present motives or reasons for cultivating it. Experience has not proven that unbelief gives strength for life's battles or wisdom for life's complexities. Unbelief is a close relative of gullibility. Unlike true faith, unbelief has a tendency toward being led by the nose by any falsehood. Unbelief yields no consolation for the present, and its outlook for the future is by no means comforting. We find no hint in the Bible of a sublime land in the clouds where people who praise their own intellectual ability will eternally baffle themselves and others. We read no prophecy in Scripture of a celestial hall of science where skeptics may weave new deceptions and forge new objections to the revelation of God. There is a place for the unbelieving, but it is not heaven.

Now, moving on to our text, in which no uncertainty is expressed, we see clearly that the Lord does not want us to be in an unsettled condition. He wants us to put an end to all uncertainty and questioning. According to the laws of men, a fact is established when an honest man has sworn to it. In the same way, we read that *"God, willing more abundantly to show unto the heirs of promise the immutability of his counsel, confirmed it by an oath."*

Accommodating the weakness of human faith, He Himself swore by what He declared and therefore gave us a Gospel that was doubly certified by the promise and the oath of the everlasting God. Surely, angels must have wondered when God lifted His hand to swear to what He had promised, and they must have concluded that, from then on, there would be an end to all strife, because of the confirmation that the Lord gave to His covenant in this way.

As we explore the meaning of the Scripture text, I must direct you to its most conspicuous metaphor. This world is like a sea—restless, unstable, dangerous, never at a standstill. Human affairs may be compared to waves driven and tossed by the wind. As for us, we are the ships that go upon the sea and are subject to its changes and motions. We are likely to be carried off course by currents, driven by winds, and tossed by storms. We have not yet come to the true *terra firma*, the dry land, which, in our metaphor, means the eternal rest that will come to the people of God. God does not want us to be *"carried about with every wind of doctrine"* (Eph. 4:14), and therefore He has been pleased to weld an anchor of hope for us that is very sure and steadfast, so that we may outride the storm.

In this passage of Scripture, I am going to focus on the set of truths that is suggested by the image of an anchor. I pray that, if you know the meaning of that anchor, you may feel it holding you securely by its grip. And if you have never possessed that anchor before, I pray that you will be enabled to cast it overboard for the first time and to feel, throughout the rest of your life, the strong comfort that such a safeguard is sure to give to your believing heart.

The Purpose of the Anchor

The purpose of an anchor, of course, is to hold a ship firmly in one place when winds and currents would otherwise move it off course or into dangerous conditions. God has given us certain truths that are intended to hold our minds securely to truth, holiness, and perseverance—to put it simply, to hold us to Himself.

To Keep Us from Shipwreck

Why does a vessel need to be held securely? The most important reason is to keep it from being shipwrecked. The ship may not need an anchor in calm waters when, on a wide ocean, a little drifting may not be a very serious matter. But there are weather conditions in which an anchor becomes altogether essential. When a gale force wind is rushing toward the shore, blowing full strength, and the vessel cannot hold its course and is in danger of being driven against the rocky coast, then the anchor is worth its weight in gold. If the ship cannot be anchored, there will be nothing left of it in a very short time except a few pieces of debris. The ship will go to pieces and every seaman will be drowned. This is the time to let down the strongest anchor and let the ship defy the wind.

Our God does not intend His people to be shipwrecked. However, we would be shipwrecked and lost if we could not be held fast in the hour of temptation. Beloved, if every wind of doctrine whirled you about at will, you would soon drift far away from the truth as it is in Jesus and your faith would be shipwrecked. But you cost your Lord too much for Him to lose you. He bought you at too great a price and values you too much to see you broken to pieces on the rocks. Therefore, He has provided a glorious safeguard for you so that when Satan's temptations, your own sinful nature, and the trials of the world attack you, hope may be the anchor of your soul, both sure and steadfast.

How much we need this anchor! We see others fall into the error of the wicked, overcome by the deceitfulness of unrighteousness and abandoned forever as castaways, *"having no hope, and without God in the world"* (Eph. 2:12).

If you have been sailing on the great waters of life for any length of time, you must be well aware that if it were not for everlasting truths, which continue to hold you securely, your spirit would quickly have been thrown into everlasting darkness long ago, and the proud waters would have gone over your soul long before this. When the mighty waves rose, it must have seemed to you as if your poor boat had gone down to the bottom of the sea, and if it had not been for the unchanging love and immovable faithfulness of God, your heart would have utterly failed. Nevertheless, here you are today, convoyed by grace, provisioned by mercy, steered by heavenly wisdom, and propelled by the Spirit's power. Thanks to the anchor, or rather to the God who gave it to you, no storm has overwhelmed you. Your ship is under way for the port of glory.

To Keep Us in Peace

An anchor is also needed to keep a vessel from distress, for even if it is not wrecked, it is a miserable thing to be driven here and there, to the north and then to the south, in whatever direction the winds may shift. Similarly, a person who is controlled by external influences is unhappy. He flies along like a feather in the breeze or rolls along the ground like something blown by a windstorm. We need an anchor to hold us so that we may remain peaceful and find rest for our souls. I praise God that there are solid and sure truths that have been infallibly certified to us. These truths operate powerfully on the mind in order to prevent it from being harassed and dismayed.

Our Scripture passage speaks of *"strong consolation."* Is that not a magnificent truth? We do not merely have a consolation that will hold us securely and bear us up against storms in times of trouble, but a *strong* consolation, so that, when trouble bursts forth with unusual strength, like a furious tornado, the strong consolation, like a powerful anchor, may be more than a match for the forceful temptation and may enable us to triumph over all. The person who has a strong belief is very peaceful.

> Hallelujah! I believe!
> Now the giddy world stands fast,
> For my soul has found an anchor
> Till the night of storm is past.

To Keep Us from Losing Ground

An anchor is also needed to keep us from losing the headway that we have made. Suppose a ship is making good progress toward its intended port but then the wind changes and blows directly at it. The vessel is in danger of being carried back to the port from which it started or to an equally undesirable port, unless it can resist the turbulent wind; therefore, it puts down its anchor. The captain says to himself, "I have made it this far and I am not going to be carried back. I am going to let down my anchor and stop here."

Believers are sometimes tempted to return to the country out of which they came, that is, to their old ways of living. They are half-inclined to renounce the things that they have learned and to conclude that they never have been taught by the Lord at all. Our old sinful nature grabs hold of us and pulls us back, and the Devil also endeavors to drive us back.

If we did not have something secure to hold onto, we would go back.

Certain cultured teachers would have us believe that there is nothing very sure. They say that, although black is black, it is not very black, and although white is white, it is not very white (and from certain standpoints, no doubt, black is white and white is black!). If it could be proven that there are no eternal realities, no divine certainties, no infallible truths, then we might willingly surrender what we know, or think we know, and wander about on the ocean of speculation as vagabonds of mere opinion. But while we have the truth, which has been taught to our own spirits by the Holy Spirit, we cannot drift from it. And we will never drift from it, even though people may consider us to be fools for our steadfastness.

Beloved, do not aspire to the kind of love and goodwill that grows out of uncertainty. There are saving truths and there are *damnable heresies* (2 Pet. 2:1). Jesus Christ is not both yes and no at the same time. His Gospel is not a deceitful mixture of the honey of heaven and the bitterness of hell, flavored to suit the taste of either good or bad. There are fixed principles and revealed facts. Those who know anything about divine things from personal experience have cast their anchors down, and when they have heard the chains going down, they have joyfully said, "I know the truth and have believed it. In this truth I stand secure and immovable. The winds may blow fiercely but they will never move me from this anchorage. Whatever I have attained by the teaching of the Spirit, I will hold onto tightly as long as I live."

The Anchor of Your Soul

To Keep Us Faithful and Useful

Moreover, the anchor is necessary so that we may be faithful and useful. The person who is easily moved and believes one thing today and another tomorrow, is fickle. Who knows where we will find him next? Of what use is he to young people or to those who are weak in faith or, indeed, to anyone else? Like a wave of the sea that is driven and tossed by the wind, what service can he give in the work of the Lord and how can he influence others for good? He himself does not believe; how can be make others believe? I think that the Christian who knows orthodox theology but who does not really believe is responsible for more unfaithfulness to God than a person who believes heresies. In other words, I am afraid that a person who earnestly believes an error has a less harmful influence on others than a person who holds the truth with indifference and with secret unbelief. The latter is tolerated in godly company, for he professes to be a believer and he is therefore able to cause harm within the body of Christ. You might say he stabs at piety beneath her shield. This person is not sure of anything; he only "hopes" and "trusts," and when defending truth, he concedes that there is much to be said on both sides, so that he kisses and stabs at the same time.

In summary, our God has provided us with an anchor to hold us securely so that we will not be shipwrecked, to keep us in peace, to prevent us from losing ground, and to enable us to remain faithful and useful. These purposes are the result of God's kindness and wisdom toward us. Let us bless the Lord who has so graciously cared for us.

The Substance of the Anchor

We must remember that making anchors is very important work. The anchorsmith has a very responsible job, for if he makes his anchor badly or of weak material, I pity the captain of the ship when a storm comes on! Anchors are not made of cast iron or of any kind of metal that happens to be handy. They are made of wrought iron, strongly welded, and of tough, compact material, which will bear all the strain that is likely to come upon them at the worst of times. If anything in this world should be strong, it should be an anchor, for safety and life often depend on it.

In the same way, we must consider what our spiritual anchor is made of. Our text reads, *"That by two immutable things, in which it was impossible for God to lie, we might have a strong consolation."* Our heavenly anchor has two great blades, made of two divine things, each of which acts as a holdfast. And, in addition to being divine, they are expressly said to be *"immutable,"* that is, they cannot change.

Two Unchangeable Things

The first blade of the anchor is God's promise, which is a sure and stable thing, indeed. We readily accept the promise of someone whom we know is an honest and reliable person. But, he may forget to fulfill his promise or may be unable to do so. Neither of these things can occur with the Lord. He cannot forget, and He cannot fail to do as He has said. What a certain thing the promise of Jehovah must be! If you only had the Lord's Word to trust in, surely your faith would never stagger.

When the Lord utters a promise, He never goes back on it, for *"the gifts and calling of God are without repentance"* (Rom. 11:29). Has he said something that He does not intend to do? Has He promised something that will not hold true? He never changes, and His promise remains from generation to generation.

The second blade of the spiritual anchor is God's oath, which is the other unchangeable thing. How could it be altered? Beloved, I hardly dare to write about this sacred topic of God's oath, His solemn assertion, His swearing by Himself! Imagine the majesty, the awe, the certainty of this!

God has pledged the honor of His name, and it is inconceivable that, under such circumstances, He will retract His commitments and deny His own declarations. On the contrary,

> The gospel bears my spirit up.
> A faithful and unchanging God
> Lays the foundation for my hope
> In oaths, and promises, and blood.

These, then, are two divine assurances, which, like the blades of the anchor, hold us securely. Who dares to doubt the promise of God? Who can have the audacity to distrust His oath?

Moreover, our Scripture passage says that it is impossible for God to lie about His promise and oath. *"In which it was impossible for God to lie."* It is inconsistent with the very idea of God that He should be a liar. A lying God would be a contradiction in terms, a self-evident incongruity. It is not possible. God must be true: true in His nature, true in His thoughts, true in His purposes, true in His actions, and certainly true in His promises and in His oath. *"In which it was impossible for God to lie."* Oh, beloved, what blessed security have we in these things! If hope cannot rest on such assurances, what can it rest upon?

The Promise

Yet, what are we really referring to when we talk about the promise and the oath? The promise is the promise given to Abraham that his seed would be blessed and that in this seed all nations of the earth would be blessed also. To whom was this promise made? Who are the seed? In the first place, the seed is Jesus, who blesses all nations. Next, the apostle Paul showed us in Romans 4:13–16 that this promise was not made to the seed according to the flesh but according to the Spirit. Who, then, are the seed of Abraham according to the Spirit? Why, they are believers, for Abraham is the father of the faithful, and God's promise, therefore, is confirmed to all who exhibit the faith of believing Abraham. To Christ Himself and to all who are in Christ, the covenant is made sure, so that the Lord will bless them forever and make them blessings.

The Oath

And what is the oath? It may refer to the oath that the Lord swore to Abraham after the Patriarch had offered up his son, which is recorded in Genesis 22:16–18. However, I think you will agree with me if I say that it more likely refers to the oath recorded in Psalm 110, which I want you to note very closely.

"The LORD *hath sworn, and will not repent, Thou art a priest for ever after the order of Melchizedek"* (v. 4). I think this is what is referred to, because the twentieth verse of our text goes on to say, *"Whither the forerunner is for us entered, even Jesus, made an high priest for ever after the order of Melchisedec."*

Now, beloved, I want you to really grasp the meaning of this anchor. One of the strong blades of the anchor is that God has promised to bless the faithful. He has declared that the seed of Abraham, namely, believers, will be blessed and will be made a blessing. The other blade of the anchor is equally strong and able to hold the soul; it is the oath of the priesthood, by which the Lord Jesus is declared to be a Priest forever on our behalf. He is not an ordinary priest like Aaron was. He did not begin and end a temporary priesthood. Instead, He is without *"beginning of days, nor end of life"* (Heb. 7:3). He lives on forever. Christ is a Priest who has finished His sacrificial work, who has gone in within the veil, and who sits forever at the right hand of God because His work is complete and His priesthood remains eternally sufficient. This is a blessed anchor for my soul: to know that my Priest is within the veil, my King of Righteousness and King of Peace is before the throne of God for me, representing me, and therefore I am forever secure in Him. What better anchor could the Comforter Himself devise for His people? What stronger comfort can the heirs of promise desire?

Our Hold on the Anchor

Notice also the hold that we ourselves have on the anchor. It would be of no use for us to have an anchor, however good it was, unless we had a firm hold on it. An anchor may be sure and may have a firm grip, but there must be a strong cable to connect the anchor with the ship. Formerly, it was very common for ships to use a fibrous cable, but large vessels are not content to run the risk of breakage. Therefore, they use a chain cable for the anchor. It is a wonderful thing to have a solid, substantial connection between your soul and your hope, to have a confidence that is truly your own, from which you can never be separated.

Our text speaks plainly about laying hold of the anchor: "[That] *we might have a strong consolation, who have fled for refuge to lay hold upon the hope set before us.*" We must personally lay hold of the hope. The hope is available but we are required to grasp it and hold it fast. With an anchor, the cable must pass through the ring in order to be bound to it. In the same way, faith must lay hold of the hope of eternal life. The meaning of the original Greek verb for *lay hold* implies, "to lay hold of our hope by strong force and to hold it in such a way that we will not lose our grip when a greater force tries to pull it from us." We must take firm hold of firm truth.

Beloved, some people have a cloudy hope, and they also seem to have a very doubtful way of laying hold of it. I suppose it is natural that it should be so. As for me, I desire to be taught something certain, and then I pray to be certain that I have learned it. Oh, to get the same kind of grip on truth as the old warrior had on his sword. After he had fought and conquered, he could not separate his hand from his sword, for his hand stuck to his sword as if it were glued to it. It is a blessed thing to get hold of the doctrine of Christ in such a way that you would have to be dismembered before it could be taken from you, for it has grown into your very self. Be sure that you have a secure hold on your sure anchor.

"But," someone may ask, "may we really lay hold of it?" My answer is that the text says it is *"set before us"* so that we may *"lay hold upon the hope."* You may grasp it, for it is set before you. Suppose you were very weak and hungry. If you came to someone's house and your host said, "Sit down," and you sat down at the table, and then he set before you a good cut of meat, some very delicious fruit, and other tasty food, would you hesitate, wondering if you could eat them? No, you would conclude that you were free to do so because your host had set them in front of you.

This is just like the invitation of the Gospel. Your hope is set before you. For what purpose is it set there? So that you may turn your back on it? Of course not. Lay hold of it, for wherever we encounter truth, it is both our duty and our privilege to lay hold of it. All the authorization that a sinner needs for laying hold of Christ is found in the fact that God has set Him forth to be the Sacrifice for our sins.

Imagine that you are on a ship in a storm and you see an anchor. Do you ask, "May I use this anchor?" No, it has been placed there for that very purpose. I guarantee you that there is not a ship captain alive who would not use an anchor during a severe storm. And he would not ask any questions about it. The anchor might not belong to the ship, it might happen to be on board as a piece of merchandise, but he would not care an atom about that. He would say, "The ship must be saved. Here is an anchor. I am going to throw it overboard." Act this way with the gracious hope that God provides for you in the Gospel of Jesus Christ: lay hold of it now and forever.

Furthermore, notice that our hold on the anchor should be a present thing and a conscious matter, for we read, *"Which hope we have."* We are conscious that we have it. No one has any right to be at peace if he does not know that he has obtained a good hope through grace. May you be able to say, "I have this hope."

Now, it is a good thing to have a cable made of the same metal as the anchor. Similarly, it is a blessed thing when our faith is of the same divine character as the truth upon which it lays hold. We need a God-given hope in order to seize the God-given promise of which our hope is made. The correct procedure is to grasp God's promise with a God-inspired confidence. In this way, it is as if, right down from the vessel to the anchor, the holdfast is one piece, so that at every point it is equally adapted to bear the strain. Oh, that we may have precious faith in a precious Christ, precious confidence in His precious blood. May God grant it to you, and may you exercise it at this very moment.

The Anchor's Hold on Us

A ship holds its anchor securely by its chain cable, but at the same time, the most important thing is that the anchor keeps its own hold on the ship. Because it has dug into the ground on the sea bottom, it holds the vessel hard and fast. Beloved, do you know anything about your hope holding you? It will hold you if it is a good hope; you will not be able to get away from it. Instead, when you are under temptation or when your spirit is depressed, when you are under trial and affliction, you will not only hold your hope, which is your duty, but your hope will hold you, which is your privilege.

When the Devil tempts you to say, "I give up," an unseen power will reply out of the infinite deeps, "But I will not give you up. I have a hold on you, and nothing will separate us." Beloved, our security depends far more on God holding onto us than on our holding onto Him. Our hope in God, that He will fulfill His promise and oath, has a mighty power over us and it is far more than equal to all the efforts of the world, the flesh, and the Devil to drag us away.

How does our divine anchor hold so firmly? *"Which hope we have as an anchor of the soul, both sure and stedfast."* It is sure regarding its own nature. The Gospel is no cunningly devised fable. God has spoken it; it is a mass of facts; it is pure, unqualified truth, and the great seal of God Himself has been set upon it. Then, too, this anchor is steadfast; it never moves from where it is lodged. It is sure in its nature and steadfast when in use, and therefore it is safe for practical application. If you have believed in Christ for eternal life and are expecting God to be as good as His word, have you not found that your hope sustains you and maintains you in your position of faith?

Beloved, the result of using this anchor will be very comfortable to you. It will not prevent you from being tossed about, for a ship that is at anchor may rock a good deal and the passengers may become very seasick, but it cannot be driven away from where it is anchored. Its passengers may suffer discomfort but they will not suffer shipwreck. A good hope through grace will not deliver you from inward conflicts altogether. More than that, it will even involve them. It also will not screen you from outward trials; in fact, it will be sure to bring them. However, it will save you from all real peril.

The condition of every believer in Jesus is very similar to that of the landlubber on board ship who, when the sea was rather rough, asked, "Captain, we are in great danger, are we not?" He received no answer, and so he said, "Captain, don't you see great fear?" Then the old seaman gruffly replied, "Yes, I see plenty of fear, but not a bit of danger." It is often that way with us; when the winds are blowing and the storms are raging, there is plenty of fear, but there is no danger. We may be greatly tossed around, but we are quite safe, for we have an anchor of the soul that is both sure and steadfast and will not move.

The Anchor's Unseen Grip

Best of all, there is the anchor's unseen grip, *"which entereth into that within the veil."* Our hope has such a grip on us that we are aware of it. It is like a boy with a kite. The kite is up in the clouds where he cannot see it, but he knows that it is there, for he feels it pull. When you are on a ship, you feel the pull of the anchor, and the more the wind rages, the more you feel the anchor holding you.

When a person can see an anchor, it is doing nothing, unless it happens to be a small anchor in shallow water. When an anchor is of use, it is gone from our sight. It has gone overboard with a splash.

Far below, among the fish, lies the iron holdfast, quite out of sight.

We cannot see our spiritual anchor, and it would be of no use if we could see it. Our good hope has gone to heaven, and it is pulling and drawing us toward itself. Its use begins when it is out of sight, but it pulls, and we can feel the heavenly pressure.

Where is your hope? Do you believe because you can see? That is not believing at all. Do you believe because you can feel? That is feeling; it is not believing. But *"blessed are they that have not seen, and yet have believed"* (John 20:29). Blessed is he who believes against his feelings, yes, and hopes against hope. It is a strange thing to hope against hope, to believe in things that are impossible, to see things that are invisible. He who can do that has learned the art of faith. Our hope is not seen; it lies in the waves, or, as the text says, *"within the veil."* I am not going to run the analogy too closely, but a seaman might say that his anchor is within the watery veil, for a veil of water is between him and it, and therefore it is concealed. This is the confidence that we have in God *"whom having not seen, [we] love"* (1 Pet. 1:8).

> Let the winds blow, and billows roll,
> Hope is the anchor of my soul.
> But can I by so slight a tie,
> An unseen hope, on God rely?
> Steadfast and sure, it cannot fail,
> It enters deep within the veil,
> It fastens on a land unknown,
> And moors me to my Father's throne.

Even though our anchor has gone out of sight, thank God that it has taken a very firm grip and *"entereth into that within the veil."* What hold can be equal to the one that a believer has on his God when he can exclaim, "You have promised. Therefore, do as You have said"?

No grasp is firmer than this: "Lord, You have sworn it, and You cannot go back on Your promise. You have said that he who believes in You is justified from all sin. Lord, I believe You. Therefore, be pleased to do as You have said. I know You cannot lie. You have sworn that Christ is a priest forever, and I am resting in Him as my Priest who has made full atonement for me. I therefore hold You to Your oath. Accept me for the sake of Jesus' sacrifice. Can You reject a soul for whom Your own Son is pleading? He is able to save to the uttermost those who come to God by Him, because He continually lives to make intercession for them (Heb. 7:25). My Lord, this is the hold that I have upon You. This is the anchor that I have cast into the deep, mysterious attributes of Your marvelous nature. I believe You, and You will not make me ashamed of my hope."

What a hold you have on the living God when you rely on His promise and oath! Therefore, you hold Him as Jacob held the angel, and you will surely win the blessing at His hands.

Note, next, that when an anchor has a good grip on the seafloor, the more the ship pulls, the tighter the anchor's hold becomes. Imagine that when the anchor goes down, it drops onto a hard rock and cannot get a grip on anything. Later on, however, it slips off the rock, lands on the bottom of the sea, and digs into the soil. As the cable draws the anchor on, the blades go deeper and deeper until the anchor almost buries itself, and the more it is pulled on, the deeper it descends. Finally, the anchor gets such a hold that it seems to say, "Now, north wind, blow all you want! You must tear up the floor of the sea before I will let the ship go."

Times of trouble send our hope deep down into fundamental truths. You may never have known affliction. If you have always been wealthy, you have never experienced need. If you have been healthy all your life, you have never gone through a trying illness. If so, you do not have half the grip on the glorious hope that those who have been tried have. Much of the unbelief in the Christian church comes out of those who profess Christ but who have never had their faith put to the test. When you have to rough it, you need solid Gospel. A hardworking, hungry man cannot live on whipped cream. He must have something solid to nourish him. In the same way, a person who is being tried feels that he must have a Gospel that is true, and he must believe that it is true, or else his soul will starve.

Now, in our Scripture text, God swore an oath, and if God swears a promise, do we not have the most solid of assurances? The righteous owe their faithful and holy God, the Three in One, no less than the firmest imaginable faith. Therefore, when greater trouble comes, believe even more firmly, and when your ship is tossed in deeper waters, believe even more confidently. When your head is aching and your heart is pounding, when all earthly joy has fled, and when death comes near, believe even more. Grow even more and more confident that your Father cannot lie. Yes, *"let God be true, but every man a liar"* (Rom. 3:4). In this way, you will receive the strong comfort that the Lord intends for you to enjoy.

Our Mediator

The text concludes with this very precious reflection, that although our hope cannot be seen, we have a Friend in the unseen land where our hope has found its hold. In anxious moments, a sailor might almost wish that he could go down to the bottom of the sea with his anchor and make sure that it is firmly secured. He cannot do that, but we have a Friend who has gone to take care of everything for us. Our anchor is within the veil; it is where we cannot see it. However, Jesus is there, and our hope is inseparably connected with His person and work.

We know for a fact that Jesus of Nazareth, after His death and burial, rose from the grave, and that forty days afterward, in the presence of His disciples, He went up into heaven. We know this as a historical fact. We also know that He rose into the heavens as the all-inclusive seed of Abraham, in whom all the faithful are found. Since He has gone there, we will surely follow, for He is the firstfruits of the full harvest.

Our High Priest

According to the text, our Lord Jesus has gone within the veil as our *"high priest."* Now, a high priest who has gone within the veil has gone into the place of acceptance on our behalf. A Melchizedek high priest is one who has boundless power to bless and to save completely. Jesus Christ has offered one bloody sacrifice for sin, namely, Himself, and now He sits forever at the right hand of God the Father. Beloved, He reigns where our anchor has entered; we rest in Christ's finished work, His resurrection power, and His eternal kingship. How can we doubt this?

Our Forerunner

We are informed next that Jesus has gone within the veil as a *"forerunner."* Why is He called a forerunner, if others are not to enter in after Him? He has gone to lead the way. He is the pioneer, the leader of the great army, the firstfruits from the dead, and if He has gone to heaven as a forerunner, then we who belong to Him will follow after Him. That reflection should make our hearts joyful.

We are also told that, as a forerunner, our Lord has entered for us. That is, He has entered to take possession in our names. When Jesus went into heaven, it was as if He looked around at all the thrones and all the palms and all the harps and all the crowns and said, "I take possession of all these in the name of My redeemed. I am their Representative and claim the heavenly places in their names." As surely as Jesus is in heaven as the possessor of all things, each one of us will also come to his inheritance in due time.

Our Lord Jesus is drawing us to heaven by His intercession. We only have to wait a little while and we will be with Him where He is. He pleads for our homecoming, and it will come to pass before long. No sailor wants his anchor to return to the ship before it is safe, for if it does so in a storm, matters look very ugly.

Our anchor will never return to us, but it is drawing us home; it is drawing us to itself, not downward beneath devouring waves but upward to ecstatic joys. Do you not feel it? You who are growing old, do you not feel it drawing you home? Many ties hold us here, but perhaps they are getting fewer with you. Perhaps your dear wife has passed away or your beloved husband is now gone. It may be that many of your children have passed away, too, as well as many of your friends. When this happens, it helps to draw us upward. If this is the case with you, I think that at this very moment you must feel as if you were about to change from a ship that floats the waters to an eagle that can fly through the air. Perhaps you have often longed to mount up on wings while singing,

> Oh that we now might grasp our guide!
> Oh that the word were given!
> Come, Lord of Hosts, the waves divide,
> And land us all in heaven!

My cable has grown shorter lately. A great many of its links have vanished. I am nearer to my hope than when I first believed; every day, my hope nears fruition. Let our joy in this state of things become more exultant. Only a few more weeks or months or years and we will dwell above. There we will need no anchor to hold us fast. However, we will eternally bless God for graciously producing such a marvelous anchor for our unstable minds while we were tossed upon this sea of care.

Think about this. What will you do if you have no anchor? A storm is coming on. I see the threatening clouds and I hear the strengthening winds of the distant hurricane. What will you do? May the Lord help you to flee for refuge immediately to the hope that is set before you in Christ Jesus.

3

Songs in the Night

God, even our own God, shall bless us.
God shall bless us.
—Psalm 67:6–7

What an extremely pleasant title: *"God, even our own God."* What loveliness and liveliness of heart must have been in the man who first applied that endearing name to the God of Jacob! Though it has been thousands of years since the sweet singer of Israel spoke of the Lord of Hosts in this way, the name has a freshness and even a novelty about it to believing ears. *"God, even our own God."* I cannot resist touching that string again, because the note is so enchanting to my soul! The words *own* and *our own* always seem to spread an atmosphere of delicious fragrance around anything with which they are connected. A poet wrote about one's own homeland in this way:

> Breathes there the man, with soul so dead,
> Who never to himself hath said,
> "This is my own, my native land"?

61

Whether it is a wasteland or a wilderness or a vast plain, all men love their own fatherland, and when they are in exile, they are smitten with home-sickness for their own country. It is the same way with regard to the houses in which we were raised. Your old homestead may have been in a poor neighborhood but still it was your own home, and a thousand kindly thoughts gather around the fireside where you snuggled beneath a parent's arm when you were a child.

Why, all our relatives are dear to us by the fact that they are our own. *Father* is a silver word at all times, but *our father, our own father*—how the name grows richer and turns to a golden word! *Our own child, our own brother, our own husband, our own wife*—the words are extremely melodious. We even feel that the Bible is all the more dear to us in our own language. The Old Testament, as the Jews' book, coming from God in Hebrew, and the New Testament, as a book for the Greeks, coming to the Gentiles in the Greek tongue, were priceless treasures. However, translated into our own familiar language and, on the whole, translated so well, our own English versions are doubly dear to us. The sweetness of the words *our own* led me to call the hymnbook from which my congregation sings, "Our Own Hymn Book," hoping that perhaps the very name might help to weave their affections around it.

But, what can I say of *"our own God"*? Words fail to express the depth of joy and delight that is contained within these three monosyllables, *"our own God."* He is our own by the eternal covenant in which He gave Himself to us, with all His attributes, with all that He is and has, to be our portion forever and ever. *"The LORD is my portion, saith my soul"* (Lam. 3:24). Also, He is *"our own God"* in the fact that we chose Him. We made this choice very freely but we were guided by His eternal Spirit, so that, while we would have chosen our own ruin, we were graciously led to choose the Lord because He had chosen us first.

He is *"our own God"*: ours to trust, ours to love, ours to run to in every dark and troublesome night, ours to commune with in every bright and sunny day, ours to be our guide in life. He is our help in death and our glory in immortality. He is *"our own God"* by providing us His wisdom to guide our path, His power to sustain our steps, His love to comfort our lives, His every attribute to enrich us with more than royal wealth. The person who can truthfully, out of a pure heart, look up to the throne of the infinite Jehovah and call Him, "my own God," has said a more eloquent thing than anything that ever flowed from the lips of the Greek orator, Demosthenes, or fell from the tongue of the Roman orator, Cicero. Those to whom *"our own God"* is a household phrase are favored beyond all other people.

> Our God! how pleasant is the sound!
>   How charming to repeat!
> Well may those hearts with pleasure bound,
>   Who thus their Lord can greet!

I think the psalmist used this expression in this sublime psalm as a kind of argument and assurance of the blessing that he foretold. *"God shall bless us"* is a true statement; it is to be believed. However, *"Our own God, shall bless us,"* is a statement that brings conviction to the most timid. It wears assurance on its forehead; it is clothed with its own evidence. If the Lord has been gracious enough to make Himself our own God, He did not do this for nothing. There is a loving intention in it. Since, in the tenderness of His compassion, He has said, *"I will be their God, and they shall be my people"* (Ezek. 37:27), it must be with the purpose of blessing us with unspeakable blessings in Christ Jesus. Underneath the surface, there is a powerful meaning that we are urged to understand in this delightful title, and the more we think about it, the more we will see it.

The words *"God shall bless us"* have been sounding in my ears like far-off bells, ringing their way with a movement of music into the depths of my soul. May the same angelic melody captivate the ears of all of my fellow believers in Christ Jesus: *"God shall bless us...God shall bless us."*

To illustrate the truth that God will bless us, I will introduce you to three personified feelings and show you how they influence our trust in God.

Fear

White-faced Fear can be found everywhere. She meddles with everything, intruding into the bedroom of Faith and disturbing the banquets of Hope. Fear stays with some people as if she were an ongoing guest and is entertained as though she were a dear, familiar friend.

What does Fear say to us in regard to our comforting Scripture text? Fear inquires, "Will God really bless us? Lately, He has withheld His hand. There have been many hopeful signs but they have disappointed us. We have been expecting the blessing for a long time, we thought we had seen signs of it, but it has not come. We have heard of revivals and rumors of revivals; men have risen up who have preached the Word of God with power, and in some places there have been many conversions. But still, to a great extent, we have not received the blessing. God has not visited us as He did in the past.

"We have seen the clouds in the morning and have expected rain. We have noticed the dew and have hoped for moisture. But these things have vanished and we are still left without the blessing. A thousand disappointments in the past lead us to fear that the blessing may not come."

My answer is this: "Listen to this, Fear, and be comforted. What if you have been too hasty and rash and have misjudged the will of the Lord? Is that any reason why He should forget His promise and refuse to hear the voice of prayer? Take an example from nature. Clouds have passed over the sky every day for many weeks now, and I have very often said, 'It will certainly rain today, and the thirsty fields will be refreshed.' Yet, not a drop has fallen, up to this point. Still, it has to rain before long.

"It is the same way with God's mercy. It may not come today, and tomorrow may not see it, but *'the Lord is not slack concerning his promise, as some men count slackness'* (2 Pet. 3:9). He has His own appointed time, and He will be punctual, for, while He is never ahead of schedule, He is never behind it. In due season, in answer to the prayers of His people, He will give them a shower of blessings. All kinds of gracious blessings will descend from His right hand. He will tear open the heavens and come down in majesty, for *'God shall bless us.'*"

"Yes," Fear replies, "but we have seen so many counterfeits of the blessing. We have seen revivals in which intense excitement has, for a while, seemed to produce great results, but the excitement has subsided and the results have disappeared. Have we not heard the sound of trumpets and the loud boasting of men again and again, and has it not only been all pride and vanity?"

What Fear says is sorrowfully true. There is no doubt that much of revivalism has been a sham. There has been much nonsense, much hot air, in the Christian church, which has been terribly harmful. The very name of *revival* has been made to stink in some places because of the dishonor associated with it. But this is no reason why a glorious and real revival should not still come from the presence of the Lord, and this is what I earnestly hope for and vehemently pray for.

Remember the revival that swept through New England in the days of Jonathan Edwards? No one could call that spurious; it was as true and real as any work of God on the face of the earth could be. Nor could anyone describe the work of George Whitefield and John Wesley as only a temporary movement or something short-lived. God was revealing Himself and working grace in a marvelous manner. Moreover, the effects of this work of God still exist today and will remain even to the coming of the Lord Jesus Christ. Therefore, we may expect that, since He already has given them at other times, God will bless His people with real and substantial advances. He will come to the front lines of battle and make His enemies see that there is an irresistible power in the Gospel of Jesus Christ.

"So, Fear, you may remember the counterfeits of the past in order to learn from them. However, do not remember them as a reason for being discouraged and depressed, for *'God, even our own God, shall bless us.'*"

"Yet," Fear replies, "see how much there is in the present that is unlike the blessing and that, instead of prophesying good, indicates evil! Only a few are proclaiming the Gospel boldly and simply. On the other hand, there are many who oppose the Gospel with their philosophies or their superstitions."

"But listen, Fear, *'God shall bless us,'* even though there may be only a few of us. God's salvation does not depend on many or few. Numbers do not matter. Remember how His servant Gideon went up to fight against the Midianites, not with thousands, for that was too many for the Lord of Hosts, but with the few hundred men who lapped the water instead of getting down on their knees to drink? And even these men did not use any weapons except broken pitchers, torches, and trumpets. Gideon defeated the multitudes of Midian with only these few things.

"Do not say that Omnipotence is short of instruments to do His will. He could make the very sand of the seashore into preachers of the Gospel if He wanted to. And if He needed tongues to tell about His love, He could make each stone a preacher or each twinkling leaf on the trees a witness for Jesus. It is not instrumentality that is necessary and of first importance. What we need most is the power that moves the instrumentality, which makes the weakest strong and without which even the strongest are weak."

I heard it said the other day that the religion of Jesus Christ cannot be expected to prosper in some places unless it has a fair start. And that remark came from someone who is supposed to be a church leader! A fair start, indeed! When you put Christianity into any arena, the only thing it asks is for the freedom to be able to use its spiritual weapons. And even where that is denied, it still triumphs. If Christianity develops its own innate strength and is left alone by the kings and princes of this world, it will work its own way.

Now, I just said that the Gospel needs to be left alone. However, let governments oppose it if they want to. Our faith will still overcome the opposition. Let them withdraw their patronage, that deadly thing that paralyzes all spiritual life, and the liberated truth of God will surely prevail. We do not tremble, then. We must not. The servants of God may be poor; they may not be gifted, they may be only a few in number. Yet, God, even our own God, *will* bless us. It does not matter if we are as few in number as the twelve apostles or if we are as uneducated as they were. They made old Rome's empire shake from end to end and brought colossal systems of idolatry down to the ground. The Christianity of today will do the same, if God returns to it in power, if, in the midst of its weakness, He valiantly fights and causes the armies of the Enemy to retreat.

But Fear always finds room for complaining. Therefore, she says, "The future, the black and gloomy future! What can we expect from this wicked generation, this perverse people, except that we will be allowed once more to be devoured by the spirit of antichrist or to be lost in the mists of unbelief?"

According to Fear, our prospects are truly appalling. However, I confess, not using her telescope,

I discern no such signs of the times. Yet Fear says so, and there may be something to it. But even if this is so, it is counterbalanced in our minds by the belief that God, even our own God, will bless us. Why should He change? He has helped His church in the past. Why not now? Is she undeserving? She has always been so. Has she backslidden? She has done so many times before, yet He has visited her and restored her. Why not now? Instead of gloomy predictions and fears, it seems to me that there is reason for the brightest expectations. But we must fall back on the divine promise and believe that God, even our own God, will bless us in our generation as He used to do in former days.

Remember the ship that was tossed by the storm on the Galilean lake? There was certainly a dreary outlook for that boat. Before long, the ship would have been driven against the rocky shore and would have sunk beneath the waves. But this was not the case, for, walking on the waves, which hardened to glass beneath His feet, was the Man who loved the group of men on that boat, and He would not allow them to die. It was Jesus, walking on the waves of the sea. He came into the vessel, and immediately the calm was as profound as if no wave had risen against the boat and no wind had blown.

In the same way, in the darkest times of the church's history, Jesus has, in due time, always appeared walking on the waves of her troubles, and then her rest has been glorious. Let us not, therefore, be afraid. Instead, throwing fear aside, let us rejoice with the most joyful expectation. What can there be to fear? *"God is with us"* (Isa. 8:10). Is that phrase not the battle cry before which demons flee and all the hosts of evil turn their backs? *"Emmanuel...God with us"* (Matt. 1:23). Who dares to stand against that? Who will defy the Lion of the tribe of Judah? They can bring their might and their spears, but if God is for us, who can be against us? Or, if any are against us, how can they stand? God is our own God. Will He let His own church be trampled in the mire? Will the bride of Christ be led into captivity? Will His beloved, whom He bought with blood, be delivered into the hands of her enemies? God forbid! Because He is God, because He is for us, because He is our own God, we set up our banners and each of us cheerfully sings:

> For yet I know I shall him praise,
>   Who graciously to me
> The health is of my countenance,
>   Yea, mine own God is he.

Desire

Now I am going to change the song altogether by introducing a second character, Desire.

Energetic, bright-eyed, and warmhearted, Desire says, "Yes, God will bless us, but if only we had the blessing now! We hunger and thirst for it. We covet it as a miser covets gold. But what kind of blessing will come and in what way will our own God bless us?"

My answer is this: "When God comes to bless His people, He brings *all* grace with Him, for in the treasures of the covenant there are not only some things, but all things; not a few supplies for some of the church's needs, but an overflowing supply from which all her needs will be replenished. When the

70

Lord blesses His church, He will give the grace of revival to all her members. They will begin to live in a higher, nobler, happier way than they have done before."

One of the highest gifts the Holy Spirit gives is to stir up the church and make her members active. This is greatly needed; I believe it is lacking among Christians today. I know certain Christians who are among the most earnest believers outside of heaven. Yet, other believers are a very long way off from that and need to be brought into a more healthy spiritual state. Many churches are too much like the foolish virgins in Matthew 25 who slept because the bridegroom did not come right away. There is too much apathy, too little love for God, too little consecration to His cause, too little grieving and longing for the souls of men. When the Lord visits His church, the first result will be the renewal of the life of His own beloved. Then the blessing will come again as people outside of the church are converted and as they are added to her membership.

I hope we will never think that God is blessing us unless we see sinners saved. Ministers are seriously deluded when they think they are prospering and yet do not see any conversions. I trust that I will be very uneasy if the number of conversions declines in my church. If God returns to His church, we will hear, to our right and to our left, "What must we do to be saved?" The astonished church will see such a multitude of children born to her, that she will exclaim in amazement, *"Who hath begotten me these?"* (Isa. 49:21) and, *"Who are these that fly as a cloud, and as the doves to their windows?"* (Isa. 60:8). When these two blessings come—an awakened

71

church and souls converted—then the word of the Lord will be fulfilled, *"The LORD will give strength unto his people; the LORD will bless his people with peace"* (Ps. 29:11).

The church will be strong; she will have the ability to refute her adversaries by pointing to her converts. She will become bold because she will see the results of her work. She will cease to doubt, for faith will be replenished with evidence. Then peace will reign. The young converts will bring in a flood of new joy; their fresh blood will make the old blood of the church leap in its veins, and old and young, rejoicing together, will delight in the abundance of peace. If you are a member of such a church, may the blessing continue and increase, and may all churches receive a blessing from the God of Israel that will make them rejoice with unspeakable joy.

Now, in spite of this, Desire says, "I see what the blessing is, but to what extent will God give it and to what degree may we expect it?"

My answer is, "God will give to you according to the amount of your confidence in Him."

We are satisfied all too soon when the blessing begins to come down from above. We stop, like Joash, the king of Israel, when we have shot only one or two arrows, and we deserve to be rebuked in the language of Elisha the prophet, *"Thou shouldest have smitten five or six times; then hadst thou smitten Syria till thou hadst consumed it"* (2 Kings 13:19). We are content with drops when we can have the cup full to the brim. We are childishly satisfied with a mere jar of water when we can have barrels and rivers and oceans, if only we have faith enough to receive them. If half a dozen people were converted in each of our churches this Sunday, we would be jubilant with thanksgiving, but should we not be sorry if there are not six hundred?

Who are we that, by our narrow expectations, we limit the Holy One of Israel? Can we draw a line around Omnipotence and say, "You may go up to this point, but no further"? Is it not wiser to extend our desires and expand our hopes, since we are dealing with One who knows no limits or boundaries? Why not look for years of plenty that will eclipse the famous seven years of plenty in Egypt during Joseph's day? Why not expect clusters of grapes that will surpass those that the Israelites found in the Promised Land? Why are we so stingy, so stunted, so narrow in our imaginations?

Let us grasp at greater things, for it is reasonable, with the Lord to trust in, to look for greater things. I picture days in which every sermon I preach will shake the building with its power, in which unbelievers will be converted to God by the thousands, as in the Day of Pentecost. Is Pentecost to be the greatest trophy of God's power? Is the first sheaf to be greater than the harvest? How can that be? We believe that if God will visit His church again, and I trust He is going to do so, we will see nations born in a day. The Gospel of Jesus Christ, which has painfully limped along like a wounded deer, will suddenly take wing like a mighty angel and fly throughout heaven proclaiming that Jesus Christ is both Lord and God. Why not? Who can justify the absence of the strongest hope, since He is able to do exceedingly abundantly above what we ask or even think?

I can hear Desire say, "Yes, I understand what the blessing is, and that it can be had in any measure, but how is it to be obtained and when will it come?"

Follow along with me in a very brief review of the psalm that is our text, because that will help us to answer the question, "When is it that *'God, even our own God, shall bless us'*?" Psalm 67 begins with *"God be merciful unto us"* (v. 1). That prayer is the voice of a repentant people confessing their past wrongs. God will bless His church when she acknowledges her faults and humbles herself; when, with a repentance in keeping with the Gospel, she stands before the mercy seat and cries out, *"God be merciful unto us."*

We must never expect the Lord to bless a proud and conceited church, a hard-hearted and indifferent church. When a church is humbled to the dust under a sense of its own shortcomings, then God will be pleased to look on it in mercy. I gather, from the context of the first verse, that God blesses His people when they begin to pray, as well as when they confess their sins. The prayer is urgent, humble, and believing; therefore, it has to speed to the throne of God. *"God be merciful unto us, and bless us; and cause his face to shine upon us"* (v. 1). These agonizing desires will be part of the mourning of a church that is conscious of having lost the blessing somewhat and that is ill at ease until it is restored. We are sure to receive the blessing from God when the entire church is interceding with urgency and persistence.

Prayer is the best resort of an earnest people. I can testify to this. In my church, we have had prayer meetings in which everyone has been stirred, much as the trees of the forest are moved in the wind, and afterward the presence of God has always been manifested by the conversion of souls. Our best times of prayer have always been followed by joyful harvests of new believers. Churches everywhere must be prayerful, intensely so, or else they cannot expect that the sound of abundant rain will be heard throughout their land. I call on the church to awake to confess her sin, to awake to struggle in prayer for the souls of men. Then the Lord God will visit us from on high. Come, Holy Spirit, and rouse Your slumbering people. Stir up the lazy multitude of believers, for when Your power is felt, then the bright day of triumph has dawned upon us.

As the psalm progresses, it speaks of praise more than it does of prayer. *"Let the people praise thee, O God; let all the people praise thee....Then shall the earth yield her increase"* (vv. 3, 6). The church needs to improve with regard to praising God. When we receive mercy, if we accept it silently and without gratitude, we cannot expect to have more. But, when every drop of favor makes us bless the Lord who gives to such undeserving ones, we will soon have more and more and more.

Praise ought to be universal: *"Let all the people praise thee."* It ought to be joyful and hearty. Each believer should rejoice in the practice of praise and put all his strength into it. When will we all wake up to this? When will all the Lord's elect magnify His glorious name as they should? When will we sing at our work, sing in our households, sing the praises of God everywhere? When prayer and praise are sacredly blended and the church becomes thoroughly eager to receive the divine blessing, then God, even our God, will bless us.

I believe that when a great visitation of mercy is coming upon the church, there are certain signs that are given to more spiritual believers, which assure them that it is coming. Elijah could hear *"a sound of abundance of rain"* (1 Kings 18:41) before a single drop had fallen, and many devout believers of God have had the conviction that a time of refreshing was coming, long before it came. Some people are especially sensitive to works of God, just as some people's bodies are especially sensitive to changes of weather before they arrive. As Columbus was sure that he was coming to land because he saw strange land birds and pieces of floating seaweed and broken wood, often a Christian minister feels sure that he is drawing near to a time of amazing blessing. He can scarcely tell others why he feels so sure, and yet to him the indications are totally sufficient.

It is as if doves come flying into our hands to tell us that the waters of indifference and worldliness are receding. They bring us olive branches, signifying that grace will surely flourish among our people, and this lets us know that the time when God is going to favor the church is indeed coming. Have you never seen the ancient prophet rise and take his harp down from the wall, begin to tune it, put every string in order, lay his fingers on the unaccustomed strings, and start to sweep the strings with unusual energy and delight? Have you never asked him, "Old harper, minstrel consecrated to the Lord, why do you strike your harp with a song that is so cheerful?" And has he not replied, "Because I see, at a great distance, the silken banners of a triumphant host returning victorious from the fight. It is the church, made more than a conqueror through Him who loves her. I hear the moving of the wings of angels; they are rejoicing over people who are repentant, and the church is glad, for her glory has returned, seeing that her sons are many." Believers who are enlightened with the light of heaven feel the shadow of the coming mercy and hear the far-off wheels of the chariot of mercy.

These signs, of course, will only be perceptible by a few, but there are other signs that may be discerned by many believers. For example, it is a very certain sign that the Lord will bless His people when they experience an unusual and insatiable craving for a divine visitation, when they feel as if the church could not go on any longer as she is now doing, when they begin to fret and pant and sigh and hunger and thirst for something better.

I pray to God that all Christians will be gloriously dissatisfied without more conversions. And when this dissatisfaction arises in the hearts of Christians, it is generally a sure indication that God is enlarging the hearts of His people so that they may receive a larger blessing. Then these prepared believers will experience sacred yearnings of intense excitement, pangs of holy purpose, mysterious longings to which they were strangers before. These will be transformed into impulses that they will be unable to resist. People who formerly could not speak about the Lord will suddenly be able to. Others who were never considered masters of intercession will become mighty in prayer. There will be tears in eyes that have been dry for a long time. We will find believers who formerly kept in the background and were never before zealous now talking to sinners and winning converts. These stirrings of God's hand, these sacred and mysterious motions of His ever blessed Spirit, are signs that He intends to bless His church to a large degree. And, beloved, when everyone begins to search within himself to see whether there is any obstacle to the blessing, when every single member of the church exposes his heart to allow God to search him and exclaims, "Take away from me everything that hinders Your work, equip me for greater usefulness, put me where You will gain glory through me, for I am consecrated to You," then we will hear the sound like *a going in the tops of the mulberry trees*" (2 Sam. 5:24), as King David did. Then we will see the flowers spring up and we will know that the time of the singing of birds is drawing near and that spring and summer are close at hand.

May God send us more and more of these gracious signs! I think I see them even now. Perhaps my wish is father to my thought, but I think I see sufficient signs that God intends to visit His church, even now. But we must believe it, we must accept it, and we must work in accordance with this expectation by praying and praising and working and striving in unity. If we do, rest assured that the year in which this occurs will be noted for such an amazing display of divine power that it will be an *annus mirabilis,* a remarkable year, a year of our Lord, a year of grace, a year whose days will be as the days of heaven on earth.

Hope

Lastly, I introduce you to a far more beautiful being than either of the other two: the sweet, bright-eyed maiden, Hope. Have you never heard the story of her matchless song? In her youth, she learned a song that she sings continually to the accompaniment of a well-tuned harp. Here are the words of her enchanting ballad: *"God shall bless us. God shall bless us."* She has often been heard singing this in the night and the stars have suddenly shone in the black sky. *"God shall bless us."* She has been known to sing this in the midst of storms and the soothing song has been followed by calm seas.

Once upon a time, certain strong laborers were sent out by a great king to level an ancient forest—to plow it, to sow it, and to bring the harvest to him. These laborers were brave and strong and willing enough for work, and they certainly needed all their strength, and more. One stalwart laborer was named Industry. His brother, Patience, with muscles of steel, went with him and did not tire in the longest days, under the heaviest labors. To help them, they had Zeal, clothed with enthusiastic and indomitable energy. Side by side worked Zeal's relative, Self-denial and his friend, Persistence. They all went out to their labor, and they took their beloved sister Hope with them to encourage them in their toils. It was a good thing that they did, for the forest trees were huge and needed many sturdy blows of the ax before they would fall to the ground. One by one, they yielded, but the labor was immense and incessant.

At night, when they went to their rest, the day's work always seemed so light, for as they crossed the threshold, Patience, wiping the sweat from his brow, would be encouraged, and Self-denial would be strengthened, for they heard a sweet voice within sing, *"God, even our own God, shall bless us. God shall bless us."* They cut down the giant trees to the music of that song; they cleared the acres one by one; they tore the huge roots from the ground; they plowed the soil; they sowed the corn; then they waited for the harvest. They were often very discouraged, but they were held to their task by silver chains and golden shackles. They were held by the sweet sound of the voice that chanted so constantly, *"God, even our own God, shall bless us."* They could never refrain from service, for Hope could never refrain from song. They were ashamed to be discouraged, they were alarmed to be despairing, for the voice rang out clearly and continually, morning and evening, *"God, even our own God, shall bless us. God shall bless us."*

You know the meaning of this parable; you recognize that voice. May you hear it in your soul today! We are few, too few for this great work, but God will bless us and therefore we are enough. We are weak and have only a little knowledge; we have little experience and slender wisdom. Yet God will bless us and we will be wise enough and strong enough. We are undeserving, full of sin, fickle, and frail; but God will bless us, and our unworthiness will be a contrast in which to set the precious diamond of His mercy. God *will* bless us—there are glorious promises that guarantee the blessing. The promises must be kept, for they are *"yea"* and *"Amen"* (2 Cor. 1:20) in Christ Jesus.

The nations must bow down before the Messiah. Ethiopia must stretch out her arms to receive her King. God will bless us. He has blessed His people. Let Egypt tell how God overthrew the enemies of His Israel. Let Canaan witness how He struck down and killed kings and overthrew mighty kings and gave their land for a heritage, a heritage for His people. God will bless us. He has given us His Son; *"how shall he not with him also freely give us all things?"* (Rom. 8:32). He has given us His Holy Spirit to remain with us forever. How can He deny us any help that we need or any essential blessing?

Our text is a song for each Christian man and woman engaged in holy work. It is a song for all the diligent teachers of Sunday school classes. If you have seen no good come out of your work and are growing somewhat discouraged, here is a psalm to raise your sinking spirits: *"God shall bless us."* Continue on and teach the Gospel to the youngsters with redoubled zeal. This is a refreshing note for the minister who has been plowing a thankless soil and has not yet seen any harvest. *"God shall bless us."* Do not cease from your energetic labors. Go back to your work, for you have such a blessing still to come that you may well rejoice even in the prospect of its coming.

Let each worker go forth to that form of Christian service to which his Master has appointed him, hearing this bird of paradise singing beautifully in his ears, *"God shall bless us."* Like David's harp playing before Saul, it drives away despair. Like the silver trumpets of the priests, it proclaims a jubilee. Oh, if only, like the rams' horns of Israel, it may level Jericho!

I want this song, *"God shall bless us,"* to stir you and move you and make you dash along like a mighty host of warriors. God is with us. He will bless us. Why do you lack enthusiasm? Why are you growing weary? Why are you looking to a human arm for strength? Why do you fear your enemies? Why are you lazy? Why are you going to bed to sleep? God will bless us. Get up, you soldiers, and snatch the victory! Farmers, gather in the harvest! Sailors, hoist your sails, for the favorable winds are coming! God *will* bless us. Oh, that fire from the altar would touch our lips (Isa. 6:5–7)! And what can be a better instrument with which to carry the flaming coal than the golden tongs of the text, *"God shall bless us"*?

Let me give you one word of warning. Suppose the Lord should bless "us" Christians, in the plural, and not "you," in the singular? What if there are showers of mercy and they do not drop on you? What if He should grant a sign for good upon His people but you are left out? It may happen, for it has happened in the past. And if this dreary possibility becomes a reality for you, it will make you worse instead of better, for, as in the story of Gideon, there is nothing as dry as the fleece that remains unmoistened when the floor is wet. There are none as lost as those who are lost while others are saved.

Be alarmed, because this could be your situation! Yet, this does not need to be the case. *"Seek ye the LORD while he may be found, call ye upon him while he is near"* (Isa. 55:6). He has abundant pardons to give, and He will give them freely to all who ask. All He requires of you is that you trust His Son. Ask the Holy Spirit to give you faith. Do trust Him! Rest upon the merit of His precious blood, and you will not be left out when He dispenses His favors. Instead, you will sing as cheerfully as all the rest, *"God, even our own God, shall bless us. God shall bless us."*

4

The Gift of Memory

This I recall to my mind, therefore have I hope.
—Lamentations 3:21

Memory is very often the servant of hopelessness. Despairing minds think about every dark prediction from the past and every gloomy aspect of the present. Memory stands like a servant, clothed in sackcloth, presenting to his master a cup of mingled wormwood and gall (Jer. 9:15). Like the mythical Roman god, Mercury, who was a messenger, he hurries, with wings on his heels, to gather fresh thorns with which to fill the pillows on which we are already sleeping uneasily and to bind fresh twigs with which to whip our already bleeding hearts.

There is, however, no need for this. Wisdom will transform memory into an angel of comfort. The same memory that may in its left hand bring so many dark and gloomy signs can be trained to carry a wealth of hopeful signs in its right hand. It does not need to wear a crown of iron; it may wear a band of gold, decorated with stars. In John Bunyon's allegorical book, *The Pilgrim's Progress,* when Christian was locked up in Doubting Castle, memory formed the club with which the famous giant beat his captives so terribly. They remembered how they had left the right road, how they had been warned not to do so, and how, in rebellion against their better natures, they had wandered into By-path Meadow. They remembered all their past misdeeds, their sins, their evil thoughts and evil words, and all these were like knots of wood in the club, causing sad bruises and wounds in their poor suffering bodies.

However, one night, the same memory that had whipped them, helped to set them free, for it whispered something in Christian's ear. He then cried out as one half-amazed, "What a fool I am to lie in a stinking dungeon when I can walk in freedom! I have a key in my inside coat pocket, called Promise. It will, I am persuaded, open any lock in Doubting Castle." So he put his hand into his coat pocket and, with much joy, he pulled out the key and thrust it into the lock. And though the lock of the great iron gate, as Bunyan put it, "went damnable hard," the key did open it and all the others, too. And so, by this blessed act of memory, poor Christian and Hopeful were set free.

Note that our text records an act of memory on the part of Jeremiah. In Lamentations 3:20 the prophet told us that memory had brought him to despair. *"My soul hath them still in remembrance, and is humbled in me."* And then, in our text, he told us that this same memory brought him life and comfort again: *"This I recall to my mind, therefore have I hope."* We may establish, then, as a general principle, that if we would exercise our memories a little more, we could, in our very deepest and darkest distresses, strike a match that would instantaneously light the lantern of comfort. God does not need to create a new thing in order to restore believers to joy. If they would prayerfully rake the ashes of the past, they would find light for the present, and if they would turn to the Book of Truth and the throne of grace, their flame would shine as before. I will apply this general principle to the situations of three kinds of Christians.

The Believer Who Is in Deep Trouble

The first is the believer who is in deep trouble. This is not an unusual circumstance for an heir of glory. A Christian is seldom at ease for very long. The believer in Jesus Christ inherits the kingdom through much tribulation. In the third chapter of Lamentations, you will observe a list of matters that memory brought before the mind of Jeremiah, and which gave him comfort. First is the fact that, however deep our present affliction is, it is by the Lord's mercy that we are not consumed (v. 22). This is a low beginning, certainly. The comfort is not very great, but when a very weak man is at the bottom of a pyramid, you must not give him a steep step at first, if he is ever going to climb it. Give him only a small stone to step on the first time, and when he gets more strength, then he will be able to take a greater stride.

Therefore, consider where you might have been. Look down through the gloomy entranceway of the grave to that realm of darkness that is like the valley of the shadow of death, full of confusion and without any kind of order. Can you discern a sound like a rushing back and forth of multitudes of guilty and tormented spirits? Do you hear their grievous crying and their frightening gnashing of teeth? Can your ears stand to hear the clanking of their chains? Can your eyes stand to see the fury of the flames? They are forever, forever, forever shut out from the presence of God and shut in with demons and despair! They lie in flames of misery so terrible that the dream of a despairing maniac cannot imagine their anguish. God has cast them away and pronounced His curse on them, appointing them to blackness of darkness forever. This might have been your fate. Contrast your present position with theirs and you have reason to sing rather than to mourn. Why should a living man complain (Lam. 3:39)?

Have you ever seen those loathsome dungeons in Venice that are below the watermark of the canal? After winding through narrow, dark, stifling passages, you may creep into little cells in which a person can scarcely stand up straight, where no ray of sunlight has ever entered since the foundations of the palace were laid. They are cold, filthy, and black with dampness and mildew, the breeding ground of fever, the place of death. And yet, those places would be a luxury to live in compared to the everlasting burning of hell. It would be an extraordinary luxury to lost spirits to lie there in lonely misery with moss growing on their eyelids, if they could only escape for a little while from a guilty conscience and the wrath of God. Friend, you are neither in those dungeons nor in hell; therefore, gather up courage, and say, as Jeremiah did in the third chapter of Lamentations, *"It is of the LORD's mercies that we are not consumed, because his compassions fail not"* (v. 22).

This may be small comfort to you. But then, if this small flame yields only a little heat, it may lead to something better. When you light a fire in your fireplace, before which you hope to sit down in warmth and comfort, you do not first expect to light the logs. You use kindling wood, and soon the more solid material gives off a pleasant glow. In the same way, this thought, which may seem so light and small, may be like the kindling of a heavenly fire of comfort for you who now are shivering in your grief.

Something better awaits us, for Jeremiah reminds us that there are some mercies, at any rate, that still continue. *"His compassions fail not. They are new every morning: great is thy faithfulness"* (vv. 22–23). You may have been reduced in wealth and you may be very poor. This is very difficult, yet be thankful if you are still in good health. Just walk into the hospital and look at the work being done there. Sit down by one patient and listen to his story of pain and weariness, and surely you will leave the hospital thinking, "I thank God that with all my poverty I do not have sickness to complain of, and therefore I will sing of the mercies that I do enjoy."

Are you sick and are you dragging your weary body around? Then I invite you to accompany me to the dark and miserable ghettos, where people languish in poverty in the heart of our cities, in wretched obscurity, and no one pities them. If you notice their hard-earned meals, too meager to yield sufficient nourishment, and the miserable dwellings that are their only rest, you will escape from the foul den of filthy poverty and say, "I will bear my sickness, for even that is better than filth, starvation, and nakedness." Your situation may be distressing, but there are others in still worse conditions. If you open your eyes and choose to do so, you can always see at least this reason for thankfulness: you have not yet been plunged into the lowest depth of misery.

There is a very touching story of a poor woman with two children who did not have a bed for them to lie on and scarcely any clothes to cover them. In the depth of winter, they were nearly frozen, and the mother took the door of a cellar off its hinges and set it up in front of the corner where they crouched down to sleep, so that some of the draft and cold might be kept from them. One of the children whispered to her when she complained of how badly off they were, "Mother, what do those little children do who have no cellar door to put up in front of them?" Even there, you see the little heart found a reason for thankfulness, and we, if we are driven to our worst extremity, will still honor God by thanking Him that His compassions do not fail but are new every morning. This, again, is not a very high step, but still it is a little farther up than the other, and the weakest may readily reach it.

Lamentations 3 offers us a third source of consolation. *"The LORD is my portion, saith my soul; therefore will I hope in him"* (v. 24). You have lost much, but you have not lost your portion. Your God is your all; therefore, if you have lost everything except God, you still have your all left, since God is all. The text does not say that God is only part of our portion but the whole portion of our spirits. All the riches of our hearts are concentrated in Him. How can we be sorrowful, since our Father lives? How can we be robbed, since our treasure is in heaven? Imagine that it is daylight, the sun is shining bright, and I am holding a lighted candle. Someone blows it out. Should I sit down and cry because my candle has been extinguished? No, not while the sun shines. God is my portion, and if I lose some little earthly comfort, I will not complain, for heavenly comfort remains.

One of the English kings, who was haughty and proud, had a quarrel with the citizens of London. He wanted to alarm the bold citizens with a terrible threat that would intimidate them. He said that if they were not careful, he would remove his court from Westminster, a borough of London. At this, the valiant Lord Mayor begged to inquire whether His Majesty meant to take away the Thames River, for as long as the river remained, His Majesty might take himself wherever he pleased.

In the same way, the world warns us, "You cannot hold out. You cannot rejoice. This trouble will come and that adversity will happen." We reply, "As long as you cannot take our Lord away, we will not complain." "Philosophers," said the wise man, "can dance without music." And true believers in God can rejoice when outward comforts fail them. The person who drinks out of the bottle, like Ishmael, the son of the slave woman, may have to complain of thirst. (See Genesis 21:9–15.) However, he who dwells at the well, like Isaac, the child of promise, will never experience need. May God grant us grace, then, to rejoice in our deepest distress, because the Lord is our sure possession, our perpetual heritage of joy. We have now advanced to some degree of hope, but there are other steps to ascend.

The prophet then reminds us of another channel of comfort, that God is always good to all who seek Him. "*The LORD is good unto them that wait for him, to the soul that seeketh him"* (Lam. 3:25). He may strike us harder than He ever has before, but if we can maintain the heavenly state of prayer, we may rest assured that He will turn from blows to kisses yet. When a beggar who is very needy sees another beggar at the door of some great man, he will watch while the other beggar knocks, and if the door is opened and the man is generously received and helped, he will knock with boldness also.

Are you very sad and depressed? The Lord is good to those who seek Him. Thousands have come from His door, but none have had any reason to complain of being given a cold reception, for in every case He has filled the hungry with good things. Therefore, go boldly and knock, for He gives liberally and does not find fault.

Prayer is an available resource for all kinds of dilemmas or difficulties. In *The Pilgrim's Progress,* when the City of Mansoul was besieged, it was in the depth of winter and the roads were very bad, but even then prayer could travel on them. I will venture to affirm that if all earthly roads were so bad that they could not be traveled, and if Mansoul were completely surrounded, so that there was not a gap left through which we could break our way to get to the king, the road upward would always be open. No enemy can barricade that; no blockading ships can sail between our souls and the haven of the mercy seat. The ship of prayer can sail through all temptations, doubts, and fears, straight up to the throne of God, and while she may have left the port with only griefs and groans and sighs, she will return loaded with a wealth of blessings. You have hope, then, for you can always pray.

The Gift of Memory

> The mercy seat is open still,
> Here let our souls retreat.

We are getting into deeper waters of joy, so let us take another step, and this time we will gain even greater comfort from the fact that it is good to be afflicted. Lamentations 3 tells us, *"It is good for a man that he bear the yoke in his youth"* (v. 27). A little child needs to be coaxed to take his medicine. He may be very sick and his mother may assure him that the medicine will cure him, but the child says, "No, it is too bitter. I cannot swallow it." Adults do not need to be persuaded in this way. The bitterness of medicine is nothing to them. They think of the health that it will bring, and so they drink it and do not even wince. Now, we may cry and murmur if we are little children and have not called to remembrance the fruit that affliction bears. But if we are adults in Christ Jesus, and have learned that *"all things work together for good to them that love God"* (Rom. 8:28), we will take the cup very cheerfully and willingly, and we will bless God for it.

Why should I dread to descend the mine shaft of affliction if it leads me to the gold mine of spiritual experience? Why should I cry out when the sun of my prosperity goes down, if in the darkness of my adversity I will be better able to count the starry promises with which my faithful God has been pleased to gem the sky? Go away, sun, for in your absence we will see ten thousand suns, and when your blinding light is gone, we will see worlds in the dark that were hidden from us by your light. Many a promise is written in invisible ink, which you cannot read until the fire of trouble brings out the letters. *"It is good for me that I have been afflicted; that I might learn thy statutes"* (Ps. 119:71). Beloved, Israel went into Egypt poor, but came out with jewels of silver and gold. The Israelites had worked, it is true, at the brick furnaces, and had suffered bitter bondage, but they were bettered by it. They came out enriched by all their tribulations.

A child had a little garden in which she planted many flowers, but they never grew. She put them in tenderly and carefully, but they would not live. Then she sowed seeds; they sprang up, but very soon they withered away. So she ran to get her father's gardener, and when he came to look at it, he said, "I will make a nice garden for you, so that you may grow whatever you want." He brought a pick, and when the little child saw the terrible pick, she was afraid for her little garden. The gardener struck his tool into the ground and began to make the earth move and shake, for his pickax had caught the edge of a huge stone that underlay almost all of the little plot of ground. All the little flowers were dug up, and the garden was ruined for a while, so that the little girl cried quite a lot. He told her he would make it a beautiful garden yet, and so he did, for, having removed the stone that had prevented all the plants from taking root, he soon filled the ground with flowers that lived and flourished. In much the same way, the Lord has come and has turned over all the soil of your present comfort to get rid of some big stone that was at the bottom of all your spiritual prosperity and would not let your soul flourish. Do not weep as the child did, but be comforted by the blessed results and thank your Father's tender hand.

One more step, and surely then we will have good ground to rejoice. The third chapter of Lamentations reminds us that these troubles do not last forever. When they have produced their proper result, they will be removed, for *"the Lord will not cast off for ever"* (v. 31).

Who told you that the night would never end in day? Who told you that the sea would recede until all that was left was a vast track of mud and sand? Who told you that the winter would proceed from frost to frost, from snow, ice, and hail to deeper snow and still more heavy storms? Who told you this? Do you not know that day follows night, that the rains come after the waters recede, that spring and summer come after winter? Then, hope! Always have hope, for God does not fail you. Do you not know that your God loves you in the midst of all this?

When mountains are hidden in the darkness of night, they are as real as they are in daylight, and God's love is as true to you now as it was in your brightest moments. No father continually disciplines. God hates the rod as much as you do. He only desires to use it for the reason that should make you willing to receive it, that it brings about your lasting good. You will yet climb Jacob's ladder with the angels and see Him who sits at the top of it—your covenant God. You will yet, amid the splendors of eternity, forget the trials of time or only remember them to bless the God who led you through them and brought about your lasting good by them. Come, sing in the night (Job 35:10). Rejoice in the midst of the flames. Make the desert blossom like the rose (Isa. 35:1). Cause the desert to resound with your exuberant joy, for these light afflictions will soon be over, and then, forever with the Lord, your bliss will never diminish!

Therefore, dear friend, memory may be, as the English poet Coleridge called it, the "bosom-spring of joy," and when the Holy Spirit bends it to His service, it may be chief among earthly comforters.

Those Who Think They Have Lost Salvation

Next, I will apply the principle of memory to the believer who thinks he has lost his salvation. It is my habit, in my ministry, to avoid extremes as much as possible and to keep to the narrow path of truth. I believe in both the doctrine of predestination and the doctrine of free will, and I follow the narrow path between those mountains. It is the same way with all other truths. I know some who think that doubts are not sins. I regret their thinking. I know others who believe that doubts are impossible where there is any faith. I cannot agree with them. I have heard of people ridiculing that very precious and admirable hymn that begins, "'Tis a point I long to know." I do not dare to ridicule it myself, for I have often had to sing it. I wish it were not so, but I am compelled to confess that doubts have troubled me. The true position, with regard to the doubts and fears of believers, is this: these things are sinful and are not to be cultivated but are to be avoided. However, most Christians, to a greater or lesser extent, do suffer them, and they are not proof that a person is destitute of faith, for the very best of Christians have been subject to them.

If you are struggling with anxious thoughts, let me urge you to call to mind, in the first place, matters of the past. Perhaps you should pause and let your heart speak to you. Do you remember the place, the spot of ground, where Jesus first met with you? Perhaps you do not. Well, do you remember happy times when He has brought you to His banqueting house? Can you remember times when He has graciously delivered you? As it says in the Psalms, *"I was brought low, and he helped me"* (Ps. 116:6) and, *"Thou hast been my help"* (Ps. 63:7). When you were in those circumstances in the past, you thought you were in overwhelming trouble. You have since passed through them. Can you find no comfort in them now?

Years ago, the sea was usually so stormy at the southern tip of Africa that when the frail sailing ships of the Portuguese went sailing south, they named it the Cape of Storms. However, after the cape had been well navigated by bolder sailors, they named it the Cape of Good Hope. In your experience, you have had many a Cape of Storms, but you have weathered them all, and now, let them be a Cape of Good Hope to you. Remember, *"Thou hast been my help, therefore in the shadow of thy wings will I rejoice"* (Ps. 63:7). Say with the psalmist, *"Why art thou cast down, O my soul? and why art thou disquieted in me? hope thou in God: for I shall yet praise him"* (Ps. 42:5).

I remember some hills like Mizar (v. 6), on which my soul has had such sweet fellowship with God that I thought I was in heaven. I remember moments of awful agony in my soul when, in an instant, my spirit leaped to the uppermost heights of ecstasy at the mention of my Savior's name. There have been times at the Lord's Table, in private prayer, and in listening to His Word, when I could say,

> My willing soul would stay
> In such a frame as this,
> And sit and sing herself away,
> To everlasting bliss.

Let me remember all these things and have hope, for,

> Did Jesus once upon me shine,
> Then Jesus is for ever mine.

God never loves and afterward hates. His will never changes. It is not possible that He who said, *"I have graven thee upon the palms of my hands"* (Isa. 49:16), should ever forget or cast away those who once were dear to Him.

Possibly, however, that may not be comforting to you. I urge you to recall the fact that others have found the Lord true to them. They cried to God, and He delivered them. Perhaps one of them was your mother. Perhaps she is now in heaven, and you are toiling and struggling onward here below. Do you not remember what she told you before she died? She said that God had been faithful and true to her. She had been left a widow when you were only a child, and she told you how God had provided for her, and for you, and the rest of your little needy family, in answer to her pleadings. Do you believe your mother's testimony? Will you not rest, with your mother's faith, upon your mother's God?

There are older Christians who could testify to you that, after fifty or sixty years in which they have walked before the Lord in the land of the living, they cannot put their finger on any date and say, "Here God was unfaithful" or, "Here He left me in my time of trouble." I am young, but I have gone through many tribulations that were painful to some degree, and I can say—and must say it, for if I do not speak, the rocks might cry out against my ungrateful silence—He is a faithful God and He remembers His servants. He does not leave them in their times of trouble. Can you also say, in the words of our text, *"This I recall to my mind, therefore have I hope"*?

Remember, and perhaps this may be a comfort to you, that although you think you are not a child of God at all now, if you look within, you will see some faint traces of the Holy Spirit's hand. The complete picture of Christ is not there, but can you not see the pencil drawing, the outline, the charcoal sketch? "What do you mean?" you ask. Do you want to be a Christian? Do you have any desire for God? Can you say with the psalmist, *"My heart and my flesh crieth out for the living God"* (Ps. 84:2)? Oh, I have had to console myself with this when I could not see a single Christian grace beaming in my spirit. I have had to say, "I know I never will be satisfied until I get to be like my Lord." *"One thing I know, that, whereas I was blind, now I see"* (John 9:25)—see enough, at least, to know my own defects and emptiness and misery. I have just enough spiritual life to feel that I want more and that I cannot be satisfied unless I have more. Well, now, where God the Holy Spirit has done as much as that, He will do more. Where He begins the good work, we are told that He will carry it on and perfect it in the Day of our Lord Jesus Christ. Call that to mind and you may have hope.

I want you to know that there is a promise in the Bible that exactly describes and suits your situation, but you must search your Bible and pray in order to discover it. There is a story that illustrates this well. A young man had been left heir to all of his father's property, but an adversary disputed his right. The case was to come to court, and while this young man felt sure that he had a legitimate right to everything, he could not prove it. His legal advisor told him that more evidence was needed than he could bring. He did not know how to get this evidence. The young man went to an old chest where his father used to keep his papers. He emptied everything out, and as he turned the writings over and over and over, he discovered an old parchment. He undid the red tape with great anxiety, and there it was, the very thing he wanted, his father's will, in which the estate was spoken of as being left entirely to him. He went into court boldly enough with that.

Now, when we get doubts, it is a good thing to turn to the Old Book and read it until at last we can say, "That is it—that promise was made for me." Perhaps it is this one: *"When the poor and needy seek water, and there is none, and their tongue faileth for thirst, I the LORD will hear them, I the God of Israel will not forsake them"* (Isa. 41:17). Or perhaps it is, *"Whosoever will, let him take the water of life freely"* (Rev. 22:17). I beg you to rummage through the Old Book. And you—poor, doubting, despairing Christian—will soon stumble on some precious parchment, as it were, that God the Holy Spirit will make for you the title deed of immortality and life.

If these memories are not sufficient for you, I have one more. I am not going to tell you something new, but still it is the best thing that was ever said out of heaven: *"Christ Jesus came into the world to save sinners"* (1 Tim. 1:15). You have heard that a thousand times, and it is the best music you have ever heard. If I am not a saint, I am a sinner, and if I may not go to the throne of grace as a child, I will go as a sinner.

A certain king was accustomed, on set occasions, to entertaining all the beggars of the city. Around him sat his royal guests, dressed in rich apparel. The beggars sat at the same table in their rags of poverty. Now, it happened that, on a certain day, one of the regular royal guests had ruined his silken clothing so that he did not dare to put it on. He felt, "I cannot go to the king's feast today, for my robe is filthy." He sat weeping until the thought struck him, "Tomorrow, when the king holds his feast, some will come as courtiers, happily clothed in their beautiful finery, but others will come and be made quite as welcome and they will be dressed in rags. "Well," he said, "as long as I may see the king's face and sit at the king's table, I will enter among the beggars." So, without mourning because he had lost his silken clothing, he put on the rags of a beggar, and he saw the king's face as well as if he had worn his scarlet and fine linen clothing. My soul has done this a great many times, and I ask you to do the same. If you cannot come as a saint, come as a sinner; only do come, and you will receive joy and peace.

In a deplorable accident that occurred in the north of England in one of the coal pits, when a considerable number of the miners were down below, the top of the pit fell in and the shaft was completely blocked up. Those who were down below sat together in the dark and sang and prayed. They gathered in a spot where the last remains of air could be breathed. There they sat and sang after the lights had gone out because the air would not support a flame. They were in total darkness, but one of them said he had heard that there was a connection between that pit and an old pit that had been worked years ago. He said it was a low passage, which a man might get through by lying flat on the ground and crawling all the way. The passage was very long, but they crept through it. At last they came out to light at the bottom of the other pit, and their lives were saved. If my present way to Christ as a saint gets blocked up, if I cannot go straight up the shaft and see the light of my Father farther up, there is an old method, the old-fashioned way by which sinners go, by which poor thieves go, by which prostitutes go.

I will crawl along humbly, flat on the ground. I will crawl along until I see my Father and exclaim, "Father, I am not worthy to be called your son. Make me like one of your hired servants, if I may only live in your house." In your worst situation, you can still come as a sinner. *"Christ Jesus came into the world to save sinners"* (1 Tim. 1:15). Call this to mind, and you may have hope.

Those Seeking God

Perhaps you are seeking God and are greatly troubled with the fear that you cannot be saved. I will give you some general truths that may give you hope.

First of all, some of you are troubled about the doctrine of election. I believe it and receive it with joy, and you may rest assured that it is true, no matter how much it troubles you. Though you may not like it, it is true. Remember that it is not a matter of opinion as to what you like or do not like, as to what you think or do not think. You must turn to the Bible, and if you find it there, you must believe it. Pay close attention to what I have to say about this. You have gotten the idea that some people will be sent to hell, simply because it is the will of God that they should be sent there. Throw the idea overboard because it is a very wicked one and cannot be found in Scripture.

Why, it would be a hell inside a man's conscience if he knew that he was condemned merely because God willed that he should be. Yet, this could never be the case, for the very essence of hell is sin, and a sense of having willfully committed it. There could not be any flames of hell if there were not this conviction in the minds of the people suffering them: "I knew my duty but I did not do it. I willfully sinned against God and I am here, not because of anything He did or did not do, but because of my own sin." Therefore, if you drive away the dark thought that God sends people to hell indiscriminately, you may be on the road to comfort.

Also, remember that whatever the doctrine of election may be or may not be, the Gospel gives a free invitation to needy sinners. *"Whosoever will, let him take the water of life freely"* (Rev. 22:17). Now, you may say, "I cannot reconcile the two." There are a great many other things that you cannot do. God knows where these two things meet, even though you do not, and I hope you do not intend to wait until you are a philosopher before you will be saved. If you do, it is likely that while you are trying to be wise by persistently remaining a virtual fool, you will find yourself in hell where your wisdom will not do you any good.

God commands you to trust Christ and promises that all believers will be saved. Leave your difficulties until you have trusted Christ, and then you will have a capacity to understand them better than you do now. In order to understand gospel doctrine, you must believe in Christ first. What does Christ say? *"No man cometh unto the Father, but by me"* (John 14:6). Election is the Father's work. The Father chooses sinners; Christ makes the atonement. Therefore, you must go to Christ, the Atoning Sacrifice, before you can understand the Father, the God of election. Do not persist in going to the Father first. Go to the Son as He tells you to.

Also, even if your own idea of the doctrine of election were the truth, you would have nothing to lose by seeking the Lord.

> I can but perish if I go,
>   I am resolved to try;
> For if I stay away I know,
>   I must for ever die.
>
> But if I die with mercy sought,
>   When I the king have tried,
> That were to die, delightful thought,
>   As sinner never died.

Trust Christ, even if you should perish, and you will never perish if you trust in Him.

Well, if that difficulty is removed, I can imagine someone else saying, "Yes, but mine is a case of great sin." Recall this to mind and you will have hope: *"Christ Jesus came into the world to save sinners; of whom,"* Paul said, *"I am chief"* (1 Tim. 1:15). Paul was the chief of sinners, and he went through the door of mercy. There can be none greater than the chief. Where the chief went through, you also can go through. If the chief of sinners has been saved, why not you? Why *not* you?

The Gift of Memory

I heard of a woman who would not cross the Salt-Ash Bridge in Plymouth, England, after it was constructed. She said she did not believe it was safe. She saw trains go over it, so that the bridge sustained hundreds of tons at a time, but she shook her head and said that she wondered how people were so immensely presumptuous as to cross it. When the bridge was totally clear and not a train was on it, she was asked if she would walk on it then. Well, she did venture a little way but she trembled the whole time, for fear that her weight would make it fall. It could bear hundreds of tons but it could not sustain her! It is much the same case with you. The stupendous bridge that Christ has flung across the wrath of God will bear the weight of your great sin, for it has already sustained ten thousand who have made it across and will bear millions of sinners yet to the shore of their eternal rest. Remember that, and you may have hope.

"But," I hear someone saying, "I believe I have committed the unpardonable sin." My dear friend, I do not believe that you have. I want you to remember one thing. The unpardonable sin is a sin that is unto death. A sin that is unto death means one that brings death on the conscience. The man who commits it never has any conscience afterward; he is dead at that point. Now, you have some feeling; you have enough life to wish to be saved from sin; you have enough life to long to be washed in the precious blood of Jesus. You have not committed the unpardonable sin; therefore, have hope. The Bible says, *"All manner of sin and blasphemy shall be forgiven unto men"* (Matt. 12:31).

But you reply, "Oh, I cannot repent, my heart is so hard." Remember that Jesus Christ has been exalted to give repentance and forgiveness of sins, and

103

you may come to Him to *receive* repentance. You do not need to bring it to Him. Come without any repentance, and ask Him to give it to you. He will give it. There is no doubt whatsoever that if the soul seeks softness and tenderness, it has that softness and tenderness to some degree even now and will have it to the fullest extent before long.

"Oh," you say, "but I have a general unfitness and incapacity for being saved." Then, dear friend, I want you to remember that Jesus Christ has a general fitness and a general capacity for saving sinners. I do not know what you need but I do know that Christ has it. I do not know the full extent of your disease, but I know that Christ is the Great Physician who can meet it. I do not know how hard and stubborn and dull and ignorant and blind and dead your nature may be, but I do know that "[Christ] *is able also to save them to the uttermost that come unto God by him*" (Heb. 7:25). What you are has nothing to do with the question, except that it is the damage to be undone. The true answer to the question of how you are to be saved lies in the bleeding body of the pure Lamb of God. Christ has all salvation in Himself. He is Alpha, He is Omega. He does not begin to save and leave you to perish, nor does he offer to complete what you must first begin. He is the foundation as well as the pinnacle. He begins with you as the green blade, and He will finish with you as the full ear of corn.

Oh, I wish I had a voice like the trumpet of God that will wake the dead at the Last Day! If I might only have it to utter one sentence, it would be this one, "Your help is found in Christ." As for you, nothing hopeful can be found in your human nature.

It is death itself; it is rottenness and corruption. Turn, turn your eyes away from this despairing mass of black depravity and look to Christ. He is the sacrifice for human guilt. His is the righteousness that covers sinners and makes them acceptable before the Lord. Look to Him as you are: black, foul, guilty, leprous, condemned. Go as you are. Trust Jesus Christ to save you, and as you remember this, you will have a hope that *"maketh not ashamed"* (Rom. 5:5), which will endure forever.

I have tried to give you words of comfort and words in season, and I have tried to express them in plain language, too. But, O Comforter, what can we do without You? You must remove our sadness. To comfort souls is God's own work. Let me conclude this chapter, then, with the words of the Savior's promise: *"And I will pray the Father, and he shall give you another Comforter, that he may abide with you for ever"* (John 14:16). And let our prayer be that He would remain with us to His own glory and to our everlasting comfort.

5

When All Looks Hopeless

Then Jesus answered...Bring him hither to me.
—Matthew 17:17

When our Lord Jesus Christ was on earth, His kingdom was so extensive that it touched the confines of both heaven and hell. We see Him at one moment discoursing with Moses and Elijah in His glory, as though He were at the gates of heaven, and then, in a few hours, we see Him confronting an evil spirit, as though He were defying the infernal pit.

It is a long journey from patriarchs to demons, from prophets to devils. Yet, mercy prompts Him and power supports Him, so that He is equally glorious in either place. What a glorious Lord He was, even while He was in His humiliation. How glorious He is now! How far His goodness reaches. Truly, He has dominion from sea to sea. His empire reaches to the extremes of human condition. Our Lord and Master hears with joy the shout of a believer who has vanquished his enemy and, at the same hour, He inclines His ear to the despairing wail of a sinner who has given up all confidence in self and desires to

107

be saved by Him. At one moment He is accepting the crown that the warrior brings Him from the well-fought fight, and at another moment He is healing the brokenhearted and binding up their wounds.

There is a notable difference between the scene of the triumphant believer who is dying and entering into his rest and the first weeping repentance of a Saul of Tarsus who is seeking mercy from the Savior whom he has persecuted. Yet, the Lord's heart and eyes are with both. Our Lord's transfiguration did not disqualify Him from casting out demons, nor did it make Him feel too sublime and spiritual to grapple with human ills. Therefore, even now, as He is at the right hand of the Father, the glories of heaven do not turn His attention from the miseries of earth, nor do they make Him forget the cries and tears of the weak who are seeking Him in this valley of tears.

The case of the deaf and mute demoniac, which is the context for the Lord's statement in our text, is a very remarkable one. All sin is the evidence that the soul is under the dominion of Satan. All who are unconverted are really possessed by the Devil in a certain sense. He has established his throne within their hearts, and he reigns there and rules the members of their bodies. *"The spirit that now worketh in the children of disobedience"* (Eph. 2:2) is the name that Paul gives to the Prince of Darkness. But these satanic possessions are not alike in every case, and the casting out of Satan, although always effected by the same Lord, is not always accomplished in the same way.

Many of us praise God that when we lived in sin, we were not given over to a passionate enthusiasm for it—there was method in our madness. We claim no credit for this but we do thank God that we were not whirled along like things that are blown in a windstorm, but were restrained and kept within the bounds of outward propriety. We are also grateful that when we were awakened and alarmed regarding our sin, and we fell under the iron rod of Satan, we were not all brought into that utter despair, that horror of great darkness, that inward tormenting agony, which some have to endure. And when Jesus came to save us, although we were greatly hindered by Satan, there was no foaming at the mouth in pride and wallowing in obstinate lust and cutting ourselves in raging desperation, analogous to the book of Mark's description of this particular incident of demon possession. The Lord opened our hearts gently with His golden key, entered the room of our spirits, and took possession.

For the most part, the conquests that Jesus achieves in the souls of His people, although accomplished by the same power, are more quietly accomplished than in the case we are considering. Let us give thanks to the God of grace for this. Yet, every now and then there are these strange, out of the way cases of people in whom Satan seems to run riot and to exert the utmost force of his malice. These are also the cases in which the Lord Jesus displays the exceeding greatness of His power, when, in almighty love, He dethrones the Tyrant and casts him out, never to return again. If there is one such distressed person reading this book, I will be justified in helping him, for,

> *if a man have an hundred sheep, and one of*
> *them be gone astray, doth he not leave the*
> *ninety and nine, and goeth into the moun-*
> *tains, and seeketh that which is gone astray?*
> *(Matt. 18:12)*

I pray that I may reach those who are far from God, and may, by the Holy Spirit's anointing, liberate those who are bound with shackles of iron so that they may become free in the Lord, for if the Son makes them free, they will be free indeed.

First, with my Lord's help, I will talk about the significance of the deplorable case recorded in the text. Then I will describe the one resource available to us and conclude by admiring the sure result.

A Hopeless Situation

The physical miracles of Christ are types of His spiritual works. The wonders that He worked in the natural world have their analogies in the spiritual world; the outward and natural are symbolic of the inward and spiritual. Now, the demoniac who was brought by his father for healing is not so distinctly representative of a case of gross sin, though the spirit is called an evil one, and Satan is always defiling, but it is an example of the great horror, disturbance of mind, and raving despair caused by the Evil One in some minds, to their torment and jeopardy.

Observe that the disease appeared every now and then in overwhelming attacks of mania, in which the man was utterly beyond his own control. The epileptic fit threw the poor victim in all directions. We have seen depressed people in whom despondency, mistrust, unbelief, and despair have raged at times with unconquerable fury. They have not so much entertained these evil guests as been victims of them. As Mark puts it, the spirit *"taketh him"* (Mark 9:18). In the same way, such forlorn ones have been captured and carried off by giant Despair. The demons have whipped them, chasing them into dry places. They have sought rest and found none. They have refused to be comforted and, like sick men, their souls have abhorred all kinds of food; they have demonstrated no power to struggle with their melancholy—they have not thought of resisting. They have been swept off their feet and carried completely out of themselves in a transport of misery. Such cases are not at all uncommon. Satan, knowing that his time is short, perceiving that Jesus is coming quickly to the rescue, lashes his poor slaves with excessive malice to see if by any means he can utterly destroy his victims before the Deliverer arrives.

The poor victim in our text was filled at times with a terrible anguish, an anguish that he expressed by foaming at the mouth, wallowing on the ground, and crying out. Sometimes, in his dreadful falls, he bruised himself, and his delirium led him to dash himself against anything that was near him, causing himself new injuries. Only those who have experienced it can describe what the pains of conviction of sin are like when they are aggravated by the suggestions of the Enemy. Some of us have gone through this to a degree, and can declare that it is hell on earth. We have felt the weight of the hand of an angry God. We know what it is to read the Bible and not find a single promise in it that would suit our situation. Instead, every page seemed to glow with threats, as if curses like lightning blazed from it. Even the choicest passages have seemed to rise up against us, as though they said, "Do not intrude here. These comforts are not for you. You have nothing to do with things such as these." We have bruised ourselves against doctrines and precepts and promises and even the Cross itself. We have prayed, and our very prayers have increased our misery. We have even fallen against the mercy seat; we consider our prayers to be only babbling sounds that are obnoxious to the Lord. We have gone to church and the preacher has seemed to frown on us and to rub salt into our wounds and to aggravate our situation. Even the Scripture reading and the hymns and the prayers have appeared to be in league against us, and we have gone home more despondent than before.

I hope you are not passing through such a state of mind as this, for it is of all things, next to hell itself, one of the most dreadful. In such a plight, men have cried out with Job,

> *Therefore I will not refrain my mouth; I will speak in the anguish of my spirit; I will complain in the bitterness of my soul. Am I a sea, or a whale, that thou settest a watch over me? When I say, My bed shall comfort me, my couch shall ease my complaint; then thou scarest me with dreams, and terrifiest me through visions: so that my soul chooseth strangling, and death rather than my life. I loathe it; I would not live alway: let me alone; for my days are vanity.* (Job 7:11–16)

I thank God that the final outcome of this slavery is often the kind that makes angels sing for joy, but while the black night endures, it is a horror of darkness, indeed. Put a martyr on the rack or even fasten him with an iron chain to the stake and let the flames burn around him. If his Lord will only smile upon him, his anguish will be nothing compared to the torture of a spirit scorched and burned with an inward sense of the wrath of God. Such a person can join in the lament of Jeremiah and cry,

> *He hath set me in dark places, as they that be dead of old. He hath hedged me about, that I cannot get out: he hath made my chain heavy. Also when I cry and shout, he shutteth out my prayer....He hath bent his bow, and set me as a mark for the arrow. He hath caused the arrows of his quiver to enter into my reins....He hath filled me with bitterness, he hath made me drunken with wormwood.*
>
> *(Lam. 3:6–8, 12–13, 15)*

"*The spirit of a man will sustain his infirmity; but a wounded spirit who can bear?*" (Prov. 18:14). To groan over unforgiven sin, to dread its well-deserved punishment, to fear everlasting burning, these are things that make men suffer intensely and make them think that life is a burden.

We learn from the text that the evil spirit, at the times when it took full possession of the man's son, sought his destruction by hurling him in different directions. Sometimes it threw him into the fire and sometimes it threw him into the water. It is the same way with deeply distressed souls. One day they seem to be all on fire with earnestness and zeal, with impatience and concern, but the next day they sink into a horrible coldness and apathy of soul, from which it appears to be utterly impossible to rouse them. All sensitive yesterday, all apathetic today. They are uncertain; you do not know where to find them. If you deal with them as you would deal with someone who is in danger from the fire of petulance, your efforts are wasted, for in the next few minutes they will be in danger from the water of indifference.

They fly to extremes. Their situation is like the fables of souls in purgatory, who suffer alternately in an oven and in cells of ice.

You would suppose, from the way in which a person like this speaks at one moment, that he believes he is the blackest of sinners, but in a short time he denies that he feels any sort of repentance for sin. You would imagine, to hear him talk at one time, that he would never cease to pray until he found the Savior, but later on he tells you that he cannot pray at all and that it is just a mockery for him to bend his knee in prayer. People like this continually change; they are more fickle than the weather. Their color comes and goes like a chameleon. They are compulsive and erratic, full of convulsions and contortions. A person would be more than human if he could know their minds for a month at a time, for they vary more often than the moon. Their conditions laugh us to scorn; their troubles baffle all our efforts at comforting them. Only Jesus Christ Himself can deal with them. It is a good thing to add that He has special skill in dealing with desperate diseases and finds delight in healing those whom all others have left for lost.

To add to the difficulties of this deplorable case, the son was deaf. Mark's account of the incident records Jesus as saying, *"Thou dumb and deaf spirit, I charge thee, come out of him"* (Mark 9:25). Because the son was deaf, there was no way of reasoning with him at all; not a sound could pass through those sealed ears. With other people, you might speak to them, and a soft word might calm the agitation of their minds. But no word, however gentle, could reach this poor tormented spirit, who was not capable of receiving either sound or sense. And are there not people like this today, to whom words are wasted breath? You may quote promises, you may supply encouragement, you may explain doctrines, but it is all nothing to them; they end where they began. Like squirrels in revolving cages, they never get anywhere.

Oh, the twisting and turning, the complex and distorted reasoning of poor tormented minds! It is certainly easy enough to tell them to believe in Jesus, but if they understand you, it is in such a vague way that it is necessary to explain it again, and you will have to clarify that explanation still further. Simply to cast themselves upon the blood of Jesus and to rest upon His finished work, is of all things most plain. A child's ABCs could not be plainer, and yet for all that, it is not clear to them. They will appear to comprehend you and then go off on a tangent; they will appear to be convinced and, for a time, to give up their doubts and fears, but meet them half an hour later and you will find that you have been speaking to a wall, addressing yourself to the deaf. Oh, what a distressing situation! May the Lord have mercy on such people, for man's help is hopeless in these cases. Praise God that He has brought help through One who is mighty, who can make the deaf hear, causing His voice to resound with sweet encouragement in the deathlike stillness of the dungeons of despair.

In addition to this, it appears that the afflicted one was mute. He was incapable of articulate speech because of the demonic possession. Since he cried out when the Devil left him, it would seem to have been a case in which all the instruments of speech were present but articulation had not been learned.

There was utterance of an incoherent sort; the speech apparatus was there, but nothing intelligible came forth except the most heartrending cries of pain.

There are many such "spiritually mute" people. They cannot explain their own condition. If they talk to you, what they say is incoherent; they contradict themselves every five sentences. You know that they are speaking what they believe to be true, but if you did not know that, you might think that they were telling you falsehoods that contradict each other. Their experience is a string of contradictions, and their speech is even more complicated than their experience.

It is very hard and difficult to talk with them for any length of time; it wears out one's patience. And if it wears out the patience of the hearer, how burdensome must it be to the miserable speaker! They pray, but they do not dare to call it prayer. Instead, to them, it is like the chattering of a seagull or a swallow. They talk with God about what is in their poor helpless hearts, but it is such a confusion and mixture of things that when they have finished they wonder whether they have prayed or not. It is the cry—the bitter, anguishing cry—of pain, but it cannot be translated into words. It is an awful groan, an unutterable yearning and longing of the Spirit (Rom. 8:26), but they themselves scarcely know what it means.

You may be weary with the details of this grievous case, but I have not yet concluded the sorrowful story. If you have never experienced anything like this, thank God for it, but at the same time, pity and pray for those who are passing through this state of mind. Appeal to God to give them the hope of the great Healer; pray that He would come and deliver them, for their plight is past the ability of man.

The father of the demoniac told Jesus that his son was wasting away. How could it be otherwise with someone who was burdened down by such a mass of afflictions, who was perpetually tormented so that the natural rest of sleep was constantly broken? It is not likely that a person's strength could be maintained for long in a system so racked and torn. Keep in mind that despair vastly weakens the soul. I have even known it to weaken the body until the worn-out sufferer has said with David, *"My moisture is turned into the drought of summer"* (Ps. 32:4).

To feel the guilt of sin, to fear the coming punishment, to have a dreadful warning in one's ears of the *"wrath to come"* (Matt. 3:7), to fear death and to expect it every moment, and above all, to disbelieve God and write bitter things against Him, this is something that makes one's bones rot and one's heart wither. John Bunyan, in his book, *Grace Abounding*, perfectly describes a person who has been left like a shrub in the desert, so that he is unable to see good when it comes. Bunyan depicts a mind that is tossed up and down on ten thousand waves of unbelief, never resting at any time but perpetually disturbed and distracted with surmises, suspicions, and foreboding. Now, if these kinds of attacks were to continue constantly and not sometimes cease, if there were not little pauses, as it were, between the fits of unbelief, surely the person's heart would utterly fail and he would die and go to his eternal home, a prey to his own cruel unbelief.

The worst point in the case of the demoniac was that all this had continued for years. Jesus asked how long he had been in this condition, and his parent replied, "Since he was a child." Sometimes God permits, for purposes that we do not understand, the deep distress of a tempted soul to last for years. I do not know for how many years a person might have to struggle, but certainly some have had to battle with unbelief until their lives were nearly over, and only in the twilight of their lives were they given faith and spiritual understanding. When they thought they must die in the dark, the Holy Spirit appeared to them and they were encouraged and comforted.

The Puritans used to quote the remarkable experience of Mrs. Honeywood as an example of the extraordinary way in which the Lord delivers His chosen. Year after year, she was in bondage to melancholy and despair, but she was set free by the gracious providence of God in an almost miraculous way. She picked up a slender piece of Venetian glassware, and saying, "I am as surely damned as that glass is dashed to pieces," she hurled it down on the floor, when, to her surprise, and the surprise of all, I do not know how, the glass was not so much as chipped or cracked. That circumstance first gave her a ray of light, and she afterward cast herself upon the Lord Jesus. Sometimes extraordinary light has been given to extraordinary darkness. God has brought the prisoner up out of the innermost cell where his feet had been securely fastened with chains, and after years of bondage, He has at last given perfect and delightful liberty.

One more thing about this case. The disciples had failed to cast the demon out. On other occasions they had been successful. They had said to their

Master, *"Even the devils are subject unto us"* (Luke
10:17). But this time they were utterly defeated.
They had done their best; they appear to have had
some faith or they would not have attempted the
task, but their faith was not at all equal to the emer-
gency. Scribes and Pharisees gathered around them
and began to mock them, and if any of the apostles
had been able to perform the deed, they would gladly
have done it. However, there they stood, defeated
and dismayed. The poor patient before them was
racked and tormented, and they were unable to give
him the slightest comfort.

It becomes a truly painful situation when an
anxious soul has gone to the house of God for years
and yet has found no consolation; when a person
who is troubled in spirit has sought but not received
help from ministers or other Christian men and
women; when prayers have been offered and not answered; when tears have been shed and have been
unavailing; when books that have been a comfort to
others have been studied without result; when
teachings that have converted thousands fail to be
effective. And yet, there are such instances in which
all human means are defeated and when it seems as
impossible to comfort the poor troubled one as to
calm the waves of the sea or to hush the voice of
thunder. There are still people in which an evil spirit
and the Holy Spirit are brought into distinct conflict,
in which the evil spirit displays all his malice and
brings the person to the uttermost height of distress,
in which, I trust, the Holy Spirit will yet display His
saving power and lead the soul out of its prison to
praise the name of the Lord.

Finding Peace in Life's Storms

If you do not know the Lord, you may be thinking to yourself, "I thank God that I know nothing about these things." Pause before you thank God for this, for as bad and deplorable as this state is, it would be better for you to be in it than to remain altogether without spiritual sensitivity. It would be better for you to go to heaven burned and branded, scourged and scarred every step of the road, than to slide gently down to hell as many people are doing—sleeping sweetly while devils carry them along the road to perdition. It is a little thing, after all, to be tormented and troubled for a time by internal distress, if, by God's intervention, it will ultimately end in joy and peace in believing. However, it is an immeasurably dreadful thing to have *"Peace, peace"* sung in one's ears *"when there is no peace"* (Jer. 6:14), and then forever to discover that you are a castaway in the pit from which there will be no escape.

Instead of being thankful, you should tremble. Yours is that terribly prophetic calm that travelers frequently perceive on the Alpine summit. Everything is still. The birds stop singing, fly low, and cower with fear. The hum of bees among the flowers is hushed. A horrible stillness rules the hour, as if death had silenced all things by stretching his awful scepter over them. Do you not perceive what is surely about to happen? The thunder is preparing; the lightning will soon cast forth its mighty fires. The earth will rock; the granite peaks will be dissolved. All nature will shake beneath the fury of the storm. That solemn calm is yours today. Do not rejoice in it, for the tempest is coming: the whirlwind and the tribulation that will sweep you away and utterly destroy you. It is better to be troubled by the Devil now than to be tormented by him forever.

The One Resource

So far, I have brought before you a very distressing subject. I pray that the Holy Spirit will help me while I remind you, secondly, of the one resource.

The disciples were baffled. The Master, however, remained undefeated and said, *"Bring him hither to me."* Now, when we are faced with difficult situations, we ought to use whatever means we have as far as the means will go. We are obligated, further, to make the means more effective than they ordinarily are. Prayer and fasting are prescribed by our Lord as the means of connecting ourselves to greater power than we would otherwise possess. There are conversions that will never happen by the methods of ordinary Christians. We need to pray more and to keep our bodies completely under control through self-denial. When we enjoy closer communion with God through prayer and fasting, we will be able to handle the more distressing cases. The church of God would have far more strength to wrestle with this ungodly age if her members prayed and fasted more often.

There is a mighty effectiveness in these two gospel ordinances of prayer and fasting. The first links us to heaven, the second separates us from earth. Prayer takes us to the banqueting table of God; fasting overturns the indulgent tables of earth. Prayer allows us to feed on the Bread of Heaven and fasting delivers our spirits from being encumbered with the fullness of bread that perishes.

When Christians raise themselves to the uttermost possibilities of spiritual vigor, they will be able, by God's Spirit working in them, to cast out demons that today, without the prayer and fasting, laugh them to scorn. But, even with all that, the most advanced Christian will still face mountainous difficulties that even prayer and fasting do not seem to alleviate. These difficulties must be brought directly to the Master and His personal skill, as the disciples discovered. The Lord tenderly commands us, "Bring them to me."

As I give you the practical application of this text, let me beg you to remember that Jesus Christ is still alive. Simple as that truth is, you need to be reminded of it. We very often estimate the power of the church by looking to her ministers, her ordinances, and her members. However, the power of the church does not lie there; it lies in the Holy Spirit and in an ever living Savior. Jesus Christ died, that is true, but He lives again, and we may come to Him today just as that anxious father did in the days when our Lord was on earth. It is said that miracles have ceased. Natural miracles may have, but spiritual miracles have not. We do not have the power to work either kind. Christ has the power to work any kind of miracle, and He is still willing and able to work spiritual miracles in the midst of His church. I do delight to think of my Lord as a living Christ with whom I can speak and discuss every situation that occurs in my ministry, a living Helper to whom I may bring every difficulty that occurs in my own soul and in the souls of others. Do not think that He is dead and buried! Do not seek Him among the dead! Jesus lives and is as able to deal with these cases of distress and sorrow as when He was here below.

Remember, too, that Jesus lives in the place of authority. When He was here, He had power over demons, but in heaven He has still greater power. Here on earth, He veiled the splendor of His divinity, but now in heaven His glory beams magnificently and all hell confesses the majesty of His power. There is no demon, however forceful, who will not tremble if Jesus merely speaks or even so much as looks at him. Today, Jesus is the Master of hearts and consciences. By His secret power, He can work upon every one of our minds; He can lower us or He can exalt us; He can cast down or He can lift up.

No situation will ever be hard for Him. We only have to bring our needs to Him. He lives—lives in the place of power—and He can achieve the desires of our hearts. Moreover, Jesus lives in the place of observation, and He still graciously intervenes. I know we are tempted to think of Him as someone far away who does not see the sorrows of His church. However, I tell you, beloved, Christ's honor is as much concerned at this moment with the defeat or victory of His servants as it was when He came down from the mountaintop and encountered the man and his demoniac son. From the battlements of heaven, Jesus looks upon the work of His ministers, and if He sees them defeated, He is jealous for the honor of His Gospel and is as ready to intervene and win the victory now as He was then. We only have to look up to our Lord. He does not sleep as the false god Baal did in the Old Testament. He is not callous to our troubles or indifferent to our griefs. Blessed Master, You are able to comfort and are strong to deliver! We only have to bring the matter that distresses us before You, and You will deal with it according to Your compassion.

We should also remember, as a warning to us, that Jesus Christ expects us to treat Him as a living, powerful, intervening One, and to confide in Him as such. We do not know what we miss through our lack of faith. We believe that certain people are in a hopeless condition, and therefore we dishonor Christ and injure them. We abandon some cases, giving up instead of presenting them constantly to Him; we limit the Holy One of Israel; we grieve His Spirit and trouble His holy mind. However, if, as children trust their fathers, we would trust in Jesus unstaggeringly, with an Abrahamic faith, believing that what He has promised He also is able to perform, then we would see even such cases as the one in our text soon brought into the light of day. The *"oil of joy"* would be given instead of mourning and the *"garment of praise for the spirit of heaviness"* (Isa. 61:3).

Now, I earnestly urge parents and relatives and any who have children or friends who are distressed, to make a point of taking their dear ones to Jesus. Do not doubt Him—you will displease Him if you do. Do not hesitate to tell Him the situation of your loved one. Hurry to Him and lay the sick one before Him. And even if, while you are praying, the case should become worse instead of better, do not hesitate. You are dealing with the infinite Son of God and you do not need to fear; you must not doubt. May God grant us grace in all aspects of our daily troubles, and especially in matters concerning our spirits, to bring everything to the Lord Jesus.

The Sure Result

When the man's son was brought before our Lord, the case looked thoroughly hopeless. He was deaf and mute; how could the Master deal with him?

124

Besides that, he was foaming at the mouth and wallowing on the ground. What opening was there for divine power? I do not wonder that his father said, *"If thou canst do any thing, have compassion on us, and help us"* (Mark 9:22). As I wrote earlier, in most other instances, the voice of Jesus calmed the person's spirit; however, that voice could not reach his mind, for his ears were sealed. The Savior had never before been presented with a more thoroughly fargone case, which was, to all appearances, hopeless; yet the cure was divinely certain, for Jesus, without hesitating for a moment, said to the unclean spirit, *"Thou dumb and deaf spirit, I charge thee, come out of him"* (v. 25). Christ has power to command demons with authority. They do not dare to disobey. The Savior added, *"And enter no more into him"* (v. 25). Where Jesus heals, he heals forever. Once the soul is brought out of prison, it will not go back again. If Christ says, "I forgive," the sin is forgiven. If He speaks peace, the peace will be like a river that never ceases; it will run until it melts away into the ocean of eternal love. There was no hope for a remedy, yet the cure was absolutely certain when Jesus put forth His healing hand. If you are broken and despondent, there is nothing that you or I can do; but there is nothing that He cannot do. Only go to Him, and with a word He will give you peace, a peace that will never be broken again but will last until you enter into eternal rest.

Nevertheless, we read that the word of Christ, though it was certain to have the victory, was staunchly opposed. The Devil had great wrath, for he knew that his time was short. He began to tear at the poor victim and to exert all his devilish force upon him. The pitiful son was foaming at the mouth and wallowing on the ground; after this terrible agitation, he fell down as if he were dead. Often, at first, the voice of Christ will cause a person's spirit to be more troubled than before, not because Jesus troubles us, but because Satan revolts against Him. A poor tempted person may even lie down in despair as if he were dead, and those around him may cry, "He is dead!" but even then the healing hand of tenderness and love will come, at whose touch the person will survive.

If, at any time, you should consider yourself to be like one who is dead, if your last hope should expire, if there should seem to be nothing before you but *"a certain fearful looking for of judgment and fiery indignation"* (Heb. 10:27), it is then that Jesus will intervene. Learn the lesson that you cannot have gone too far from Christ. Believe that your limits are only limits to you and not to Him. The highest sin and the deepest despair together cannot baffle the power of Jesus. If you were between the very jaws of hell, Christ could snatch you out. If your sins had brought you even to the gates of hell, so that the flames flashed into your face, if you then looked to Jesus, He could save you. If you are brought to Him when you are at death's door, eternal mercy will still receive you. How is it that Satan has the impudence to make men despair? Surely it is a piece of his infernal impertinence that he dares to do it. Despair, when you have an omnipotent God to help you? Despair, when the precious blood of the Son of God has been given for sinners? Despair, when God delights in mercy? Despair, when the silver bell of hope rings, *"Come unto me, all ye that la-*

bour and are heavy laden, and I will give you rest" (Matt. 11:28)? Despair, while life lasts, while mercy's gate stands wide open, while the messengers of mercy call you to come? Despair, when you have God's word, *"Though your sins be as scarlet, they shall be as white as snow; though they be red like crimson, they shall be as wool"* (Isa. 1:18)?

I repeat, it is infernal impertinence that has dared to suggest the idea of despair to a sinner. Christ unable to save? It can never happen. Christ outdone by Satan and by sin? Impossible. A sinner with diseases too many for the Great Physician to heal? I tell you that if all the diseases of men were concentrated in you, and all the sins of men were heaped on you, and blasphemy and murder and fornication and adultery and every sin that is possible or imaginable had all been committed by you, the precious blood of Jesus Christ, God's dear Son, would still cleanse you from all sin. If you will only trust my Master—and He is worthy to be trusted and deserves your confidence—He will save you even now. Why delay, why raise questions, why debate, why deliberate, mistrust, and suspect? Fall into His arms. He cannot reject you, for He Himself has said, *"Him that cometh to me I will in no wise cast out"* (John 6:37).

Only the Master can save you. It is my responsibility to tell you about the Gospel, but I know that you will not hear it, or that, if you do hear it, you will reject it unless Christ comes with power by His Spirit. Oh, may He come today and say to the evil spirit within you, "Come out of him, you foul spirit, and do not return to him. Let him go, for I have redeemed him with My most precious blood." I pray, dear friend, that God the Holy Spirit may bless these words so that the bars of iron may be unfastened, the gates of brass may be opened, and the captives of the Enemy may be brought out to liberty. May the Lord bless these captives for His name's sake.

6

Christ in You

And hope maketh not ashamed; because the love of God is shed abroad in our hearts by the Holy Ghost which is given unto us.
—Romans 5:5

Pentecost is repeated in the heart of each believer when the love of God is poured out into his heart by the Holy Spirit. Let me give you a little bit of historical analogy to illustrate this. The Lord's disciples were deeply sorrowful when He died on the cross. The distress that came upon them as they thought of His death and His burial in Joseph's sepulcher was very painful. But after a little patience and experience, their hope revived, for their Lord rose from the dead and they saw Him ascend into heaven. Their hopes were bright concerning their Lord who had gone into glory and had left them a promise that He would come again and cause them to share in His victory. After that hope had been conceived in them, they were, in due time, made partakers of the Holy Spirit, whose divine influence was poured out on them so that they were filled with His power. They were made bold. They were not ashamed of their hope but proclaimed it through the preaching of Peter and the other disciples. The Holy Spirit had visited them and therefore they fearlessly proclaimed to the world the Lord Jesus, their *"hope of glory"* (Col. 1:27).

Truly, history repeats itself. The history of our Lord is the foreshadowing of the experience of all His people. What happened to the Firstborn happens, to some degree, to all the children of God. We have an excellent example of this in the first part of Romans 5, from which our text comes. Verse three mentions our tribulation—our agony, our crossbearing. The passage goes on to say that out of our patience and experience a blessed hope arises in due season. We are renewed by our Lord's resurrection life and come out of our sorrow. He raises us up from the grave of our affliction. Then we receive the divine visitation of the Holy Spirit, and we enjoy our Pentecost: *"The love of God is shed abroad in our hearts by the Holy Ghost which is given unto us."* I trust you know what this means and are now enjoying it.

As a result of that visitation by the Holy Spirit, our hope becomes clear and assured and we are led to give a full and bold testimony concerning our hope and the blessed One who is the substance of it. I hope that you have already proven that you are not ashamed. If not, I hope you will do so. Our God has visited us in mercy and endowed us with the Holy Spirit, who is His choice Gift to His children. The Holy Spirit dwelling in us has caused us to know and feel the love of God, and now we cannot help speaking and telling others about what the Lord has made known to us. Thus, on a small scale, we have repeated a portion of early church history in our own personal story. You will find that, not only in this case, but in all cases, the life of the believer is the life of Christ in miniature. He who originally said, *"Let us make man in our image"* (Gen. 1:26), still follows the model of Christ when making a person into a *"new creature"* (2 Cor. 5:17) in the image of His Son.

Now let us examine some of the mystery of our spiritual experience. The passage in Romans 5 that I mentioned above is like a little map of the inner life:

> *Tribulation worketh patience; and patience, experience; and experience, hope: and hope maketh not ashamed; because the love of God is shed abroad in our hearts by the Holy Ghost which is given unto us.* (Rom. 5:3–5)

This passage can only be fully understood by people of God who have had it written in capital letters on their own hearts. *"Tribulation worketh patience,"* said the apostle. This is not true in the natural. Normally, "Tribulation worketh impatience," and impatience misses the fruit of experience and sours into hopelessness. Ask many who have buried a dear child or lost their wealth or suffered pain in their bodies, and they will tell you that the natural result of affliction is to produce irritation against providence, rebellion against God, questioning, unbelief, faultfinding, and all sorts of evils. But what a wonderful change takes place when the heart is renewed by the Holy Spirit! Then, but not until then, *"tribulation worketh patience."*

He who is never troubled cannot exercise patience. Angels cannot exhibit patience since they are not capable of suffering. In order for us to possess and exercise patience, it is necessary for us to be tried, and a great degree of patience can only be obtained by a great degree of trial. You have heard of the patience of Job. Did he learn it among his flocks or with his camels or with his children when they were feasting? No, truly, he learned it when he sat among the ashes and scraped himself with a piece of broken pottery and when his heart was heavy because of the death of his children. Patience is a pearl that is only found in the deep seas of affliction; and only grace can find it there, bring it to the surface, and adorn the neck of faith with it.

Then, patience provides us with personal experience in learning the character of God. In other words, the more we endure and the more we test the faithfulness of God, the more we prove His love and the more we perceive His wisdom. He who has never endured may believe in the sustaining power of grace, but he has never experienced it. You must put to sea to know the skill of the divine Pilot, and you must be battered by the storm before you can know His power over winds and waves. How can we see Jesus in His full power unless there is a storm for Him to calm? Our patience works in us an experiential acquaintance with the truth, the faithfulness, the love, and the power of our God. We bow in patience, and then we rise in the joyful experience of heavenly support. What better wealth can a person have than to be rich in experience? Experience teaches. This is the real school for God's children. I hardly think that we learn anything thoroughly without the rod of affliction. Certainly we know best the things that have been a matter of personal experience. We need that truth to be burned into us with the hot iron of affliction before it can be of use to us. After that, no one may trouble us, for our hearts bear the brand of the Lord Jesus. This is the way in which patience works experience.

It is rather extraordinary that the Scripture then says that experience works hope. It is not extraordinary in the sense of being questionable, for there is no hope as bright as that of the believer who knows the faithfulness and love of God through experience. But does it not seem extraordinary that this heavy tribulation, this grievous affliction, this painful chastisement, should nevertheless bring forth for us this particular bright light, this morning star of hope, this messenger of the everlasting day of glory? Beloved, divine chemistry wonderfully brings out fine gold from metal that we thought was worthless!

The Lord in His grace spreads a bed for His own people on the threshing floor of tribulation, and there, like Boaz in the book of Ruth, we take our rest. He sets to music the roar of the floods of trouble. Out of the foam of the sea of sorrow He causes the bright spirit of hope that *"maketh not ashamed"* to arise. Therefore, this passage, from which our text comes, is a choice extract from the inner life of a spiritual man. It is a fragment of the mystery of our spiritual lives. We must read it with spiritual understanding.

Now, our text describes none other than the house of God and the gate of heaven. You can see in it a temple for the worship of the Divine Trinity. Read both the fifth and sixth verses of Romans 5, and notice that all three members of the Trinity are mentioned:

> *The love of God* [the Father] *is shed abroad in our hearts by the Holy Ghost which is given unto us. For when we were yet without strength, in due time Christ died for the ungodly.*

The blessed Three in One! The Trinity is needed to make a Christian, the Trinity is needed to encourage a Christian, the Trinity is needed to complete a Christian, and the Trinity is needed to create in a Christian the hope of glory.

I always like these passages that bring us so near to the Trinity. They make me want to adore the Godhead in the words of the doxology:

> Glory be unto the Father, and to the Son,
> and to the Holy Ghost.
> As it was in the beginning, is now,
> and ever shall be, world without end!
> Amen

It is a very dear thing to be called upon to offer special worship to the one true God, the Three in One, and to feel one's heart readily inclined to do so. By faith, we bow with the multitudes of the redeemed before the all-glorious throne and worship Him who lives forever. We adore Him wholeheartedly when we think of the unity of the Sacred Three in our salvation! Divine love is bestowed on us by the Father, made manifest in the death of the Son, and poured out into our hearts by the Holy Spirit. Oh, to feel communion with the Triune God! Let us bow before the sacred majesty of Jehovah, and as we explore our text, let us allow the Holy Spirit to teach us its truths so that through it, we may enter His temple.

The text reads: *"Hope maketh not ashamed; because the love of God is shed abroad in our hearts by the Holy Ghost which is given unto us."* The apostle had been progressing until he came to the hope of

134

glory. When he reached that height, he could not help saying something concerning it. Turning away from his main subject, as was often his custom, he gave us a few glowing sentences about the believer's hope.

He first explains the confidence of our hope—that *"hope maketh not ashamed."* Next, he describes the reason for our confidence, which I hope you are enjoying today, for we are confident that we will never be disappointed in our hope because the love of God has been poured out into our hearts by the Holy Spirit. Then, he reveals the result of this confident hope, that we are not ashamed of the Gospel of Christ and that we are witnesses to the world.

The Confidence of Our Hope

Some people have no hope, or they have a hope of which they might justifiably be ashamed. Ask those who deny the validity of the Scriptures what their hope for the future is. "I will die like a dog," they will answer, "and when I am dead, that will be the end of me." If I had such a wretched hope as that, I certainly would not go around the world proclaiming it. I would not think of gathering a large audience and saying to them, "Friends, rejoice with me, for we are to die like cats and dogs." It would never strike me as being a matter to celebrate.

The agnostic knows nothing, and therefore I suppose that he hopes for nothing. I do not see anything to become enthusiastic about in this stance, either. If I had no more hope than that, I would be ashamed. The Roman Catholic's best hope is that when he dies he may come out all right in the end, but meanwhile he will have to undergo the purging fires of purgatory. I do not know much about that place, for I cannot find any mention of it in Holy Scripture. However, those who know it well, because they invented it and keep its keys, describe it as a dreary place, to which even great bishops and cardinals must go. I have seen, personally seen, invitations to the faithful to pray for eternal rest for the spirit of an eminent cardinal; and if this is the fate of the princes of the church, where must ordinary people go? There is no great excellence in this hope. I do not think I would call people together in order to say to them, "Rejoice with me, for when we die we will all go to purgatory." They would fail to see any particular grounds for rejoicing. I do not think I would say much about it, and if anybody were to question me about it, I would try to evade the point and declare that it was a deep mystery that would be better left to the clergy.

But we are not ashamed of our hope. We believe that Christians who are absent from the body are present with the Lord (2 Cor. 5:8). We look for a city that has foundations, whose Builder and Maker is God (Heb. 11:10). We are not ashamed to hope for glory and immortality and eternal life.

Not Ashamed of the Object of Our Hope

Moreover, we are not ashamed of the object of our hope. We do not believe that heaven consists of indecent, carnal pleasures. We do not believe in an Islamic paradise of sensual delights, or we might very well be ashamed of our hope. Whatever imagery we may use, heaven is a pure, holy, spiritual, and refined happiness. The false prophet would not have regarded this as a sufficient bait for his followers. Yet, our hope is this: that our Lord will come a second time with all His holy angels, and *"then shall the righteous shine forth as the sun in the kingdom of their Father"* (Matt. 13:43). We believe that if we die before that time, we will sleep in Jesus and will be blessed with Him. *"To day shalt thou be with me in paradise"* (Luke 23:43) is not for the thief only, but for all of us who have entrusted our spirits to the crucified Savior. At His coming we expect a glorious resurrection. When He descends from heaven with a shout, with the voice of the archangel and the trumpet of God, then our spirits will be restored to our bodies and we will live with Christ as complete, renewed persons. We believe, and are sure, that from that day we will be with Him forever. He will grant us the right to share in His throne, His crown, and His heaven—forever and ever! The more we talk about the promised bliss, the more we feel that we could not possibly be ashamed of the hope of glory.

The ultimate reward of faith, the ultimate reward of a life of righteousness, is such that we rejoice in the prospect of it. Our glorious hope includes purity and perfection: freedom from all sin and the possession of every virtue. Our hope is that we will be like our perfect Lord and that we will be with Jesus where He is so that we may see His glory. Our hope is fulfilled in this promise, *"Because I live, ye shall live also"* (John 14:19). We will not merely exist, but *live,* which is another and a higher matter. Our life will be the life of God in our spirits forever and ever. We are not ashamed of this hope. We press forward to attain it.

Not Ashamed of the Ground of Our Hope

Our hope rests on the solemn promises of God, which He has made to us by His prophets and apostles and confirmed in the person and work of His dear Son. Since Jesus Christ died and rose from the dead, we who are one with Him by faith are certain that we will rise again from the dead and live with Him. The fact that Christ was resurrected is our assurance that we will be resurrected, and His entrance into glory is the pledge of our glorification, because we have been made one with Him by the purpose and grace of God.

We all fell with Adam because all humanity is born in him. In the same way, we will rise and reign with Jesus because we are now in Him. God is not the God of the dead but of the living; He *is* the God of Abraham, Isaac, and Jacob, and therefore these men are still alive. We believe the same thing concerning all who die in the faith, that they have not ceased to be but are all alive in Him. Our hope is not established on reasoning, which may possibly, in a dim way, prove the immortality of the spirit and the future reward of the righteous. Rather, our hope is founded upon the Word of God, which states the truth of eternal life clearly and plainly and leaves no room for doubt. If the Bible is a lie, we must give up our hope; however, since we have not followed *"cunningly devised fables"* (2 Pet. 1:16) but have received the testimony of faithful eyewitnesses to our Lord's resurrection and ascension, we believe the Holy Record and are not ashamed of our hope. What God has promised is sure, and what God has done fully confirms it. Therefore, we have no fear.

Not Ashamed That We Possess Our Hope

Now, somebody may say to us with a sneer, "So, you expect to be in glory, do you?" Our reply is, "Yes, we do, and we are not ashamed to receive the mild accusation you bring, for our confidence is well grounded. Our expectation is not based on any proud claim of personal merit but on the promises of a faithful God. Let us recall some of these promises. He has said, *"He that believeth on me hath everlasting life"* (John 6:47). We do believe in Him, and therefore we know that we have eternal life. He has declared in His Word that *"whom he justified, them he also glorified"* (Rom. 8:30). We are justified by faith; therefore, we will be glorified. Our hope is not based on mere feeling but on the fact that God has promised everlasting life to those who believe in His Son, Jesus Christ. We have heard our Lord pray, *"Father, I will that they also, whom thou hast given me, be with me where I am; that they may behold my glory"* (John 17:24). We believe that the Father has given us to Jesus because we have been led to put our trust in Him, and faith is the sure sign and symbol of divine election. Therefore, since we are Christ's, we expect to be with Him where He is.

We also read in the Word of the Lord, *"Whosoever believeth in him should not perish, but have everlasting life"* (John 3:16), and therefore we hold onto that promise and know that we have everlasting life. This appears to be a strictly logical argument. Unless it is a mistake and God has not said that the believer will live forever, we are under no delusion in expecting eternal life. But God's Word is the surest thing there is, and we are not ashamed to hold onto any claim that truthfully arises out of it. We dare to believe that God will keep His word to us and to all other believers.

Not Ashamed regarding the Certainty of Our Hope

In addition, beloved, we are not ashamed of the absolute certainty that our hope will be realized. We believe that if, indeed, we are justified by faith and have peace with God, we have a hope of glory that will not fail us in the end or on the way to the end. We do not expect to be deserted and to be left to fall from grace, *"for he hath said, I will never leave thee, nor forsake thee"* (Heb. 13:5). We do not expect to be left to ourselves, which would mean our sure and certain ruin, but we do expect that He who has begun a good work in us will perfect it until the Day of Christ. We are certain that He who has created this hope in us will justify that hope by fulfilling it in due time. He will preserve us through long life if we are to live a long time; He will maintain a living hope in us when the time comes for us to die; and He will remember even our dust and ashes when they are hidden in the grave. *"Who shall separate us...from the love of God, which is in Christ Jesus our Lord?"* (Rom. 8:35, 39). It is written, *"He that believeth and is baptized shall be saved"* (Mark 16:16). And this is the way it will be. The believer will not *"perish from the way"* (Ps. 2:12) or during the way. Has God not said, *"I will put my fear in their hearts, that they shall not depart from me"* (Jer. 32:40)? He will not allow His children to stumble and fall. He says, *"I give unto [my sheep] eternal life; and they shall never perish, neither shall any man pluck them out of my hand"* (John 10:28). We will never be deceived in our trust in Jesus. No one will be able to say, "I trusted the Lord Christ to keep me, and He has not kept me. I rested in Jesus to preserve my spiritual life, and He has not preserved me." Never. We will not be ashamed of our hope.

The Reason for This Confidence

I have introduced you to the confidence that makes believers—especially tried and experienced believers—full of the hope that *"maketh not ashamed."* My second purpose is to focus on the reason for this confidence. Why do believers who possess the good hope rejoice in it?

The Love of God

One of the main supports of this hope is the love of God. I expect one day to sit among the angels and to see the face of my Best Beloved. I do not expect this because of anything in me or anything that may ever be done by me but simply because of the infinite love of God. I do not trust my love for God, only God's love for me. We trust Him because He loves us. We are sure that He will fulfill our hope because He is too loving to fail us.

It is from the love of God that all our hopes begin and it is upon the love of God that all our hopes depend. If it were not for the Father's love, there never would have been a covenant of grace. If it were not for His infinite love, no atoning sacrifice would have been provided. If it were not for His active love, no Holy Spirit would have given us life and renewed us. If it were not for His unchanging love, all that is good in us would soon pass away. If it were not for love almighty, love unchangeable, love unbounded, we could never hope to see the face of the King in His beauty in the land that is very far off. He loves us, and therefore He leads us and feeds us and establishes us forever. Does your heart not confess this? If that love could be suspended for a moment, if it were to cease sustaining you for an instant, where would you be? The love of God is the chief reason for our hope in Him.

Observe, dear believer, that the actual reason for our confidence is that *"the love of God is shed abroad in our hearts by the Holy Ghost."* The Holy Spirit is in the heart of every believer and He is occupied with many acts of grace. Among other things, He pours out the love of God in the hearts in which He resides. Let me give you an illustration of this. Suppose that an ornate box filled with precious perfume is placed in a room. The dormant scent is contained within the box. It is an exquisite perfume, but no one has yet breathed in its fragrance. The love of God that comes into the believer's heart is like that rare fragrance; until it is poured out, it is not enjoyed. The Holy Spirit takes that box and opens it, and the sweet scent of divine love streams forth and completely fills the believer. This love penetrates, permeates, enters, and occupies his entire being. A delightful scent streams through an entire room when the fragrance of roses is poured out. In the same way, when a devout believer reflects on the love of God, and the Holy Spirit helps his meditations, the theme fills his mind, memory, imagination, reason, and emotions. It is an engrossing subject and is not to be confined to any one faculty, any more than you could keep the aroma of spices within a certain narrow space.

Moreover, as perfume delights the sense of smell, the love of God, when poured out in the power of the Holy Spirit, imparts an extraordinary sweetness to our emotions. All the garments of the Lord of love smell of myrrh and aloes and cassia (Ps. 45:8). What sweetness can be compared to the love of God? That the eternal and infinite One should really love mankind, and love it to such a degree as He has done, is a truth that is at once surprising and joyful. It is the root from which the lily of perfect joy springs. This is an ivory palace in which every resident is made glad. You may meditate on that love until you are overcome and carried away by it, and until your soul, before you are aware of it, becomes like *"the chariots of Amminadib"* (Song 6:12).

Also, perfume not only permeates the air and delights all who are in the room, but it remains there. You may take the perfume away, but a sweet scent remains for many hours in a room that was once filled with it. Some scents seem to stay forever. Perhaps you went to your dresser drawer the other day and noticed a delicious scent of lavender, yet you had not had a sachet in there since last year. Fragrance lingers. A few drops of a pure fragrance will perfume a wide area and remain long after the bottle from which they were poured has been taken away.

When the love of God comes into the heart and is poured out by the Holy Spirit, who is the great Master of the art of diffusing love, it remains in the heart forever. Everything else may cease, but love remains. For a moment we may seem to forget the love of God when we are in the midst of the business of the world, but as soon as the pressure is removed, we return to our rest. The sweet perfume of divine love overcomes the rank odor of sin and never abandons the heart that has known its excellent delights.

If I may change the analogy, the love of God that is poured out in the heart by the Holy Spirit is like a rain cloud, black and full of overflowing blessings, which pours out a shower of innumerable silver drops that fertilize every place that they fall, making drooping plants lift up their heads and rejoice in the heaven-sent revival. After a while, a gentle steam rises from the spot where the rain fell, which ascends to heaven and forms fresh clouds. The love of God is poured into our hearts in the same way and permeates our natures until our spirits drink it in and its new life produces flowers of joy and fruits of holiness. Later on, our grateful praise ascends like the incense that smoked on Jehovah's altar in the temple. Love is poured out in us and it works upon our hearts to love in return.

Leaving these analogies, the shedding abroad of the love of God into the heart by the Holy Spirit means this: He gives us an intense appreciation and sense of that love. We have heard of it, believed in it, and meditated upon it. Finally, we are overpowered by its greatness. *"God so loved the world, that he gave his only begotten Son"* (John 3:16). We cannot measure such love. We become affected by it; we are filled with wonder and admiration. Its greatness, its uniqueness, it distinction, its infinity—all these amaze us. It is poured out into our hearts.

Then we truly begin to take personal possession of His love. We exclaim, "He loved *me*, He gave Himself for *me*." We begin to feel that God's love was not only love for men in general but love for us in particular, and we are now completely swept off our feet. When we believe in this special love for us, we are ready to dance for joy. Faith perceives that it is true, and then we *"praise* [the Lord] *upon the high sounding cymbals"* (Ps. 150:5). This is followed, as a matter of course, by a giving back of love, which the human heart must feel. We love Him because He first loved us. We doubted it once; we cannot doubt it now.

If we were to be asked three times, as Peter was, *"Lovest thou me?"* (John 21:15), we would answer humbly but most emphatically, *"'Thou knowest all things; thou knowest that I love thee'* (v. 17). Lord, I could not live without loving You. I would a thousand times rather that I had never been born than be without love for You. Although I do not love You as I ought to and my heart desires a far greater love for You, I do love You in deed and in truth. You know that I do, and I would be false to my own conscience if I denied it." This is what it means to have the love of God poured out in your heart by the Holy Spirit who has been given to us: to know it, enjoy it, appropriate it, rejoice in it, and come under its divine influence. May this sweet perfume never be removed from my innermost soul!

Christ Died for the Ungodly

Next, I want you to notice the special sweetness that struck the apostle Paul as being so amazingly noteworthy. He went on to tell us what affected him most. He said, *"When we were yet without strength, in due time Christ died for the ungodly"* (Rom. 5:6).

That is the second point to be considered, that God would give His Son to die for the *ungodly*. The fact that God would love those who love Him, that God would love His renewed people who are striving for holiness, is indeed delightful, but the most overpowering thought of all is that He loved us when there was nothing good in us whatsoever. He has loved us since before the foundation of the world. He saw that we were fallen and lost, and His love resolved to send His Son to die for us. Jesus did not come because we were good but because we were evil. He did not give Himself for our righteousness but for our sins. What motivated God to act in love was not any excellence in His human creation that existed at that time or was foreseen to exist in the future, but simply the good pleasure of the God of love. Love was born of God Himself. It was so great in the heart of God that

> He saw us ruined in the fall,
> Yet loved us notwithstanding all.

He loved us when we hated Him; He loved us when we opposed Him, when we cursed Him, when we persecuted His people and blasphemed His ways. What a marvelous fact! Oh, that the Holy Spirit would bring home that truth to our hearts and make us feel its energy! I cannot possibly express the immensity of God's love for you, much less pour it out within you, but the Holy Spirit can do it, and then how captivated you will be, how humbled and yet how full of praise you will be for the Most High God!

Therefore, the apostle was not content to remind us of God's immense love for us. He also did not want us to forget that Christ died for us. Beloved, that

Christ should love us in heaven was a great thing; that He should then come down to earth and be born in Bethlehem was a greater thing. That He should live a life of obedience for our sakes was a wonderful thing, but that He should die, this is the climax of love's sacrifice, the summit of the mountain of love.

Some sights in the world astonish us once or twice and then grow commonplace. However, the Cross of Christ grows on us; the more we know of it, the more it surpasses knowledge. To a believer who has been saved for two thousand years, the sacrifice of Calvary is even more of a marvel than when he first saw it. That God Himself should take our nature and that, in that nature, He should die a death like a felon who is put on display on an execution post, in order to save us who were His enemies, is a thing that could not be believed if it had been told to us on any less authority than God's. It is altogether miraculous, and if you will let it take possession of you until it is poured out in your heart by the Holy Spirit, you will feel that there is nothing worth knowing, believing, or admiring compared to this. Nothing can ever rival our interest in the Cross of Christ. We may study many fields of knowledge, but the knowledge of a crucified Savior will still remain the most sublime of all the sciences.

Christ Will Save Us by His Life

Furthermore, the apostle went on to say that the Lord must forever love us now that we are reconciled. He put it in this way: If God loved us when we were His enemies, He will surely continue to love us now that we are His friends. If Jesus died for us when we were rebels, He will refuse us nothing now that He has reconciled us. If He reconciled us by His death, surely He can and will save us by His life (Rom. 5:10). If He died to reconcile enemies, surely He will preserve the reconciled.

Do you see the whole argument? It is very full of reasons for upholding our hope of glory and causing us not to be ashamed of it. When the great God makes us feel the surpassing greatness of His love, we banish all doubt and dread. We infer from the character of His love, which we have seen in the past, that He cannot possibly abandon us in the future. What, die for us and then leave us? What, pour out His heart's blood for our redemption and yet permit us to be lost? Will Jesus, robed in the crimson of His own atonement through death, manifest Himself to us—something He does not do to the world—and then, after all this, say to us, *"Depart from me, ye cursed"* (Matt. 25:41)? Impossible! He never changes. Our hope has, for the keystone of its arch, the unchanging love of Jesus Christ, who is the same yesterday and today and forever. The Holy Spirit has poured out the love of God in Christ Jesus into our hearts in such a way that we feel quite sure that nothing can separate us from it. And as long as we are not divided from it, our hope of glory is as sure as the throne of the Eternal.

The apostle also reminded us that *"we have now received the atonement"* (Rom. 5:11). We already feel that we are one with God. Through the sacrifice of the Lord Jesus, we are at peace with God. We love Him; our quarrel with Him has ended. We delight in Him; we long to glorify Him. Now, this delightful sense of reconciliation is a satisfactory assurance of grace and glory. The hope of glory burns in the golden lamp of a heart that has been reconciled to God by Jesus Christ. Since we are now in perfect accord with God, longing only to be and to do just what He would have us to be and to do, we have the beginnings of heaven within us, the dawn of the perfect day. Grace is glory in the bud. Agreement with God is the seed of perfect holiness and perfect happiness. If we are under the dominion of holiness, if there is nothing that we would continue to hold onto if we knew that it was contrary to the mind of our holy Lord, then we may be assured that He has accepted us and that we have His life in us and will finally come into His glory. He who has caused His enemies to become His wholehearted friends will not permit this gracious work to be undone or His holy purpose to fail. Our present delight in God is the pledge of our endless joy in Him. Therefore, we are not ashamed of our hope.

The Holy Spirit Is Working in Us

One more thought about this. Note well that the apostle not only mentions the love of God and the fact that it has been poured out into our hearts, but he also mentions the divine Person by whom this has been accomplished. The pouring out of God's love into our hearts has been brought about by the Holy Spirit who has been given to us. This could have been done only by the Holy Spirit. Would you ever have been captivated by the love of God through the influence of the Devil? Would you ever have been overpowered and filled with excessive joy in the love of God through the power of your own fallen human nature? Judge for yourself! Those who have felt the love of God poured out into their hearts can say without a doubt, "This is the finger of God; the Holy Spirit has worked this in me." Nothing short of the Holy Spirit can effect it. Someone may say, "Thank God that I have had the privilege to hear powerful preaching!" That may have been the case, and yet you may never have felt the love of God within your heart. Preachers can shed love abroad by preaching, but they cannot shed it abroad in people's hearts. A higher influence than human oratory must deal with the inner nature.

Perhaps you were alone in your room or walking by the roadside when the sweet savor of love stole into your heart. Oh, the love of God! The amazing, immeasurable, incomprehensible love of the Father! Oh, to feel this until our very souls are inflamed with it and our unloving nature is all on fire with love for the great Lover of the souls of men! Who can do this except the Holy Spirit? And how did we come to have the Holy Spirit except by the free gift of God, whose gifts and calling *are without repentance*" (Rom. 11:29)? God does not give and then take; His gifts are ours forever. If the Holy Spirit has been given to you, is He not the pledge of God's love? Does the New Testament not describe Him as the deposit, the downpayment of the inheritance? Is a deposit not the security for all the rest? Would the Holy Spirit set His seal to a document which, in the end, would prove to be so faulty that it could not effect its purpose? Never. If the Holy Spirit dwells in you, He is the guarantee of everlasting joy. Where grace is given by His divine indwelling, glory must follow. When the Holy Spirit comes into a person, He comes to make His home. He will remain in us until we are caught up to the higher realms to see our Lord's face forever.

The Result of Our Confident Hope

This confident hope produces inward joy. The person who knows that his hope of glory will never fail him because of the great love of God that he has tasted, will hear music at midnight. The mountains and the hills will break out into singing wherever he goes. He will be found rejoicing *"in hope of the glory of God"* (Rom. 5:2), especially in times of tribulation. His most profound comfort will often be enjoyed in his deepest affliction, because then the love of God will be especially revealed in his heart by the Holy Spirit, whose name is the *"Comforter"* (John 14:16). Then he will perceive that the rod of correction has been dipped in mercy, that his losses have been sent in fatherly love, and that his aches and pains have been measured out with gracious purpose. In our affliction, God is doing nothing to us that we would not wish for ourselves if we were as wise and loving as God is. My friend, you do not need gold to make you happy; you do not even need health to make you glad. If you will only get to know and feel divine love, the fountains of delight will be poured out to you— you will be introduced to the banquets of happiness.

Our inward joy brings with it the grace of holy boldness in the declaration of our hope. Christians do not show unbelievers the joy of their hope often enough. We do not wear our best uniforms or say enough of the joy of being in the Lord's service or speak enough of the wages that our Lord will pay at the end of the day. We are as silent as if we were ashamed of our hope. We even go around mourning, although we have reason to be the happiest people on God's earth. I am afraid that we do not have enough experience of having had divine love poured out into our hearts. If the perfume were within us, it would be perceived by those who are around us. When you pass a perfume factory, you immediately perceive the sweet scent. Let us cause unbelievers to know the fragrance of our joyous hope. Let us especially tell those who seem most likely to laugh at us, for I have learned by experience that some of these are most likely to be affected.

Many times a new convert has written to an unbelieving friend to tell him of his great change and of his new joy, and that friend has put the letter aside with a sneer or a joke. However, after a while he has thought it over and has said to himself, "There may be something in this. I am a stranger to the joy of which my friend speaks, and I certainly need all the joy I can get, for I am dejected enough." Let me tell you that all unbelievers are not the fools that some would take them to be. They are aware of an unrest within their hearts, and they hunger for something better than this empty world can give them. Because of this, it frequently happens that as soon as they learn what is good, they accept it. Even if they are not hungering for God, I do not know any better way of making someone long for food than for you yourself to eat. The onlooker will feel his mouth water and will suddenly get an appetite.

In the parable of the prodigal son, the servants were ordered to bring out the best robe and to put it on him, to put a ring on his hand and shoes on his feet. However, the father did not tell them to take the son and make him eat. What he said was, *"Let us eat, and be merry"* (Luke 15:23). He knew that when his hungry son saw others feasting, he would start eating, too. When those who belong to the divine family eat and drink in happy fellowship, and are merry with the Lord in feasting upon divine love, the poor hungry brother will desire to join you, and he will be encouraged to do so.

May we enjoy true godliness so much that we never bring shame upon it or feel shame concerning it. Come, then, you who have a hope of glory, let all men see that you are not ashamed of it. Act as decoy birds to others. That is, let the sweet notes of your happy lives attract them to Jesus! May the Lord cause you to disperse the love that He has poured out into your hearts, and may that which perfumes your hearts also perfume your houses, your businesses, your conversations, and your entire lives! Let all who meet you see *"Christ in you, the hope of glory"* (Col. 1:27).

All of Grace
Charles H. Spurgeon

Charles Spurgeon outlines the plan of salvation in such clear, simple language that everyone can understand and be drawn to the Father. Any attempt to please God based upon our own works brings only self-righteousness and coldness of heart, but God's free grace makes the heart glow with thankfulness for His love. This classic is summed up in Spurgeon's final cry to the reader, "Meet me in heaven!"

ISBN: 978-0-88368-857-1 • Trade • 176 pages

WHITAKER HOUSE

www.whitakerhouse.com

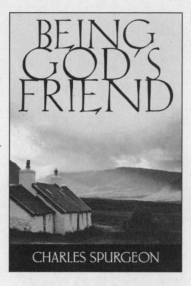

Being God's Friend
Charles H. Spurgeon

You know Him as God, Yahweh, the Almighty, Lord.
Sometimes He's even Father, Abba, Daddy.
But do you know Him as Friend? Do you love to
spend time with Him? Do you look forward to
your conversations, to your quiet times together?
You can have dynamic fellowship with the Father,
with greater purpose and power than ever before.
Experience the closeness and joys of an
intimate friendship with God.

ISBN: 978-0-88368-723-9 • Trade • 192 pages

WHITAKER
HOUSE
www.whitakerhouse.com

Grace and Power
Charles H. Spurgeon

Do you long to become the person God wants you to be? Do you wish you had more spiritual power? You can experience victory over sin, forgiveness and freedom from guilt, and a positive understanding of your salvation. Here is a dynamic collection of six of Charles Spurgeon's books, filled with biblical insights that will transform your life. It is possible to trade your weakness for God's strength and power—by His grace!

ISBN: 978-0-88368-589-1 • Trade • 624 pages

WHITAKER HOUSE

www.whitakerhouse.com

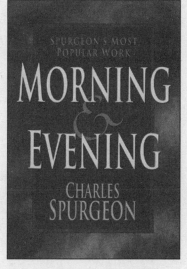

Morning and Evening
(revised edition)
Charles H. Spurgeon

"Encouraging thoughts are like honey to the heart," says Spurgeon, whose uplifting messages for each day of the year will bring comfort and refreshment to your walk with God. Whether you spend your time alone with God in the morning or the evening, or both, Spurgeon's message will powerfully affect your life, inspire your faith, and fill your heart with a profound sense of peace and joy.

ISBN: 978-0-88368-749-9 • Trade • 752 pages

WHITAKER HOUSE
www.whitakerhouse.com

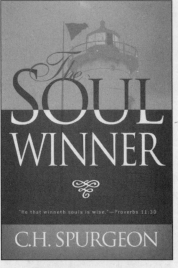

The Soulwinner
Charles H. Spurgeon

When Jesus returned to heaven, He left us with a mission—continue His work of bringing lost souls home to the Father. Charles Spurgeon accepted this mission and personally escorted thousands of people into the saving knowledge of Jesus Christ. In this book, he crystallizes the wisdom and experience of a lifetime as a soulwinner.

"If you are eager for real joy, I am persuaded that no joy of growing wealthy, no joy of influence over your fellow creatures, no joy of any other sort, can ever compare with the rapture of saving a soul from death."
—C. H. Spurgeon

ISBN: 978-0-88368-709-3 • Trade • 304 pages

WHITAKER HOUSE
www.whitakerhouse.com

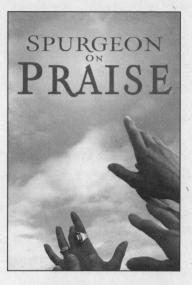

Spurgeon on Praise
Charles H. Spurgeon

Teaching out of long experience and a rich understanding of Scripture, Charles Spurgeon shows that praise is an important part of a balanced Christian life. He explains why we should praise the Lord, different kinds of praise, how attitudes affect our ability to praise, how praise and prayer are related, and the strength of a thankful heart. Spurgeon says that praising God should be a regular habit of every believer. Find out why, and how, you can deepen your relationship with God through praise!

ISBN: 978-10-60374-042-5 • Mass Market • 224 pages

WHITAKER
HOUSE

www.whitakerhouse.com

Spurgeon on Prayer and Spiritual Warfare
Charles H. Spurgeon

Here is a beloved treasury of six of Charles
Spurgeon's best-selling books. Many keys to living
a successful Christian life can be found in these
practical yet anointed words—keys to praying,
praising, and warring against Satan. Victory in Christ
can be yours as you implement these vital truths.
Answered prayers and a deeper faith in God await
you, so what are you waiting for?

ISBN: 978-0-88368-527-3 • Trade • 576 pages

WHITAKER
HOUSE
www.whitakerhouse.com